WOMEN
inside

WOMEN INSIDE

The experience of women remand prisoners in Holloway

Silvia Casale

With a Foreword by
Gordon H. Lakes, CB MC

The Civil Liberties Trust

The Civil Liberties Trust

The Civil Liberties Trust (formerly the Cobden Trust) is a registered charity established in 1963 to seek the protection and extension of civil liberties in the United Kingdom by researching the causes of injustice and educating the public about their rights and responsibilities.

How you can help

We depend on generous public support to do our work. As a registered charity, the Trust can recover tax from the Inland Revenue on any covenanted donation. If you would like to help us in this way, or would like further information, then please write for details to the Secretary, The Civil Liberties Trust, 21 Tabard Street, London SE1 4LA.

The Civil Liberties Trust
21 Tabard Street
London SE1 4LA

The Trust's publications do not necessarily reflect the views of the Trust.

ISBN 0 900137 30 4

© Silvia Casale 1989

BRITISH LIBRARY CATALOGUING-IN-PUBLICATION DATA

Casale, Silvia
  Women Inside: the experience of women remand
  prisoners in Holloway
  1. England. Women Prisoners. Prison Life
  I. Title II. Civil Liberties Trust
  365'.43'0942

ISBN 0 900137 30 4

Designed by Paula McDiarmid
Typeset by Wordsmiths Typesetting Limited
Printed by Lithosphere Printing Co-operative Limited

ACKNOWLEDGEMENTS

A great many people, some of whom cannot be named, helped to make this study possible. I thank them all for their time, interest and advice.

I would like to thank the London Borough of Islington Council's Women's Committee and Women's Support Unit for funding the project and in particular Hilary Potter for her help. The Noel Buxton Trust and the Eva Reckitt Trust generously provided additional funds and without Jerry Katzman's continuing support the project would not have been possible.

I am grateful to Anthony Langdon for his interest and help in getting the research off the ground; and to the Prison Department for granting me access to prison establishments and consistently facilitating all aspects of the research with openness and efficiency.

Sarah Spencer, Sara Huey, Christine Jackson and Gerard Duveen of the Civil Liberties Trust have helped in the task of translating the research into this report. I thank them sincerely for their efforts and commitment to the project.

Elaine Player gave valuable advice in the design stage and thereafter; Chris Tchaikovsky of Women in Prison shared her insights and expertise. I received much valuable information from Nicky Vassell at the Women Prisoners' Resource Centre, Jill Matthews, Clare Gregory and Paul Cavadino at NACRO, Jenny Hicks at CAST and William Bingley at MIND. I thank them all for their help.

I greatly appreciate the advice of Vivien Stern at NACRO, Stephen Shaw and Una Padel of the Prison Reform Trust, and Frances Crooke of the Howard League who read and made helpful comments on the manuscript.

Successive governors of Holloway, Joy Kinsley and Colin Allen, generously allowed me to work in Holloway and I am grateful for their trust and support. I would like to thank Colin Allen for inviting me back to Holloway to see the changes which have taken place there and for including me in discussions about future change.

My thanks also to the Governors of H.M. Prisons Styal and East Sutton Park and to their staff for welcoming me and allowing me to talk with women prisoners transferred there. The experience and knowledge of members of staff were valuable in comparing their establishments with Holloway

At Holloway I owe a special debt of gratitude to Margaret Smith and Ingrid Posen for sharing their expertise and easing my passage. Robin Sewell, John Shine, Angela Town, Richard Brown and Norman Hindson have all contributed information and explanations which have helped my understanding of Holloway. I am grateful to all the women and men staff working in Holloway who tolerated my presence and assisted the work with patience and understanding.

Finally my thanks to the women prisoners who talked to me about themselves. I cannot name them, but I hope that they will see themselves in these pages and feel that it was worth sharing their time inside with me.

Silvia Casale

Dr. Silvia Casale has worked in criminal justice in the USA and Sweden. She is an independent criminologist and a member of the Parole Board. Her books include *Minimum Standards for Prison Establishments* (NACRO 1984) and *The Fine Process* (Vera Institute 1985).

Foreword

The prison system is seriously overcrowded: in April 1988 the population was 5,000 above the normal accommodation level. The overcrowding is not evenly distributed across the whole of the prison system but is at its worst in the local prisons and remand centres where, during 1987-88, an average of 22,500 prisoners occupied accommodation designed for fewer than 16,000. It is in these establishments that nearly 11,000 men and women, who are either unconvicted or unsentenced, are held on remand. In 1987 the magistrates' courts remanded a total of 42,900 people in custody.

Women prisoners form only a small proportion of the total prison population. They accounted for only 3.5% of the adult prisoners under sentence on 30 June 1986 and for 4.8% of those received into custody on remand during that year. Unlike their male counterparts, the majority of women remanded in custody do not subsequently receive a prison sentence. This study confirms that many remands in custody are not for serious offences by people who are a real risk to society. With the present level of overcrowding in our local prisons and remand centres this is a matter of real concern on logistical as well as humanitarian grounds.

Although this book is about women remanded in custody, many of the issues discussed are relevant to all remand prisoners. Until recently the remand population has been relatively neglected both by research and in the general debate on the management of the prison system, its organisational structure and the development of regime activities for prisoners. When people refer to prisons they tend to think only of places where prisoners serve their sentences, forgetting or not knowing that about one fifth of the prison population is on remand. Similarly, the Prison Service has tended to define its work with the sentenced prisoner primarily in mind, work with remand prisoners being seen as mainly concerned with providing services to the courts.

This report argues convincingly that greater attention should be paid to the different and special obligations and functions associated with the custody and care of remand prisoners. It makes a case for a re-orientation of approach which acknowledges and responds to the distinct status, legal rights and needs of remand prisoners. A good deal of work has already been done to define more clearly the tasks of the Prison Service and more is being done to develop performance indicators which will enable the quality of service to be more accurately assessed. It is important that this monitoring process is further refined to measure the quality of service provided to individual prisoners and not only the average provision which can, of course mask gross inequalities.

The remand focus is particularly relevant to the current debate on privatisation stimulated by the Government's Green Paper, 'Private Sector Involvement in the Remand System'. Before the state can delegate to private agencies its obligations and functions relating to the care of remand prisoners, those obligations and functions need to be clearly defined and required standards of service established to safeguard the special position of the individual remanded in custody. The Green Paper recognises the importance of clear and enforceable standards if private agencies are to take on the care and control of remand prisoners.

A basis for the formulation of standards already exists in official documents such as the Prison Rules, Standing Orders and Circular Instructions, as well as the general guidance contained in the United Nations Standard Minimum Rules and the more recently revised European Prison Rules. At present they are neither readily available nor easily accessible as a consolidated package either for contractual purposes or for day to day use by staff and prisoners.

The arbitrariness of control in prison, to which Dr Casale refers, is often directly related to the paucity of unambiguous and generally available rules governing the behaviour of both staff and prisoners. The research clearly illustrates how daily life in prison is regulated by many *ad hoc* rules of dubious authority which can damage the relationship between staff and prisoners.

The research upon which this book is based was carried out at a time of great upheaval as the transition from the old to the new Holloway was nearing completion. Since that time a great many changes have been made and the quality of life for prisoners has been improved in a number of respects. Much still needs to be done but it is significant that both the former and the present Governor invited Dr Casale to continue visiting and to join in discussions about current and future changes in the prison. I can think of no better testimony to the thoroughness and sensitivity with which the research was conducted and to its relevance to contemporary problems. Both policy-makers and practitioners will benefit from a study of this work.

Gordon H. Lakes CB MC

Contents

Introduction 1

Chapter 1
Theories and facts 7

Chapter 2
Case related problems of women on remand 25

Chapter 3
Personal needs and problems of women on remand 43

Chapter 4
Special care 75

Chapter 5
Conclusions: Implications of the study for
changes in policy and practice 97

Selected Bibliography 117

Introduction

Objectives

This study examines the experience of women remanded in custody before conviction and between conviction and sentence. It seeks to identify the problems faced, and posed, by women on custodial remand and the effects of imprisonment upon their ongoing court cases, their personal lives within and beyond the prison system and their special care needs.

The underlying purpose is to identify the civil liberties implications of the remand in custody of women defendants and offenders and to suggest changes in policy and practice. The focus on remand prisoners does not imply that civil liberties issues are less relevant for sentenced prisoners nor that recommendations for change should be implemented at the expense of sentenced prisoners.

The report is based on original research undertaken at H.M. Prison Holloway by permission and co-operation of the Home Office Prison Department and the Governor, who provided information and allowed access to the staff, the prisoners and the Holloway files on women prisoners. The research is placed in the context of current ideas and assumptions about the imprisonment of women on remand.

Until recently there has been relatively little consideration of the overwhelming importance of gender to an understanding of criminal behaviour. Consequently studies of those accused or convicted of criminal involvement have been heavily influenced by the prevalence of men among this population both in terms of recidivism and gravity of offending behaviour.

The present study is part of a shift of attention in recent years towards the problems faced and posed by women in the criminal justice system. Since women are so dramatically under-represented among those involved in crime, not only in sheer numbers but also as serious or persistent offenders, it follows that few women should find themselves at the extreme of the criminal justice process: in prison. Yet many of the women who end up in prison do not belong to that small minority involved repeatedly in grave offences. Many lack a long serious record and are involved in non-violent, even relatively trivial offences.

Moreover women are not generally in prison as a result of conviction or sentence. Many are awaiting trial, while some are convicted but awaiting reports before sentencing. This is probably the most glaring and least investigated fact about the female prison population. Most men, who go to prison before conviction or sentence, end up sentenced to prison and serving additional time. Often their time on custodial remand will be offset against their sentence. Most women who go to prison do not end up serving a prison sentence. Many are there only as defendants, or as offenders about whom the court wants more information and, in most cases, the court will eventually impose a non-custodial sentence.

This phenomenon raises serious questions: why are so many women, relatively speaking, remanded in custody when they will not receive a prison sentence? Why is there so high a rate of women remanded for reports, especially medical reports?

The primary focus of this study is the prison system. It therefore cannot provide direct answers about why women are found in the prison system, although, by using a number of research methods to examine the characteristics of women remanded in custody and the anomalies and inequities of their position, it provides information which challenges the rationality not only of the prison system but also of the court process.

Approach

The study combines a number of research strategies. It places the original data in context by providing a brief overview of the literature on women in the criminal justice system and the information currently available from official sources and research. The original data are derived almost entirely from research at Holloway, with a small amount of additional research on women passing through the remand stage and to allocation at two other prisons: Styal, a closed establishment, and East Sutton Park, an open establishment. The follow-up material was collected primarily for comparative purposes: to crystallise the analysis of the remand experience at Holloway through the contrast with other prisons.

Holloway is inevitably a major subject of interest for any study of women in prison, by virtue of its size, mixture of remand and sentenced prisoners and specialist functions. For a study of women in custody it is an obvious choice. However, research previously undertaken at Holloway[1] has not focused primarily on the remand population, even though it represents an important group both numerically and because of the anomalies associated with women's remand. Unlike their male counterparts, women remand prisoners are not sent to local prisons, but housed in a few facilities, often at great distances from their families and friends.

Methods of Research

The main research in Holloway took place over the course of ten months, from September 1984 to June 1985, with follow-up at Styal and East Sutton Park. The core information came from documents, observation and interviews on and with three samples of women prisoners in Holloway:

Sample A: thirteen women remanded before trial
Sample B: thirteen women remanded before sentence
Sample C: eight women in Holloway as sentenced prisoners

The considerable waiting times before trial and, to a lesser extent, between conviction and sentence, together with the many mechanical problems of selecting and locating women prisoners on remand made it impracticable to track a single sample of women over time through the successive stages of the system, i.e. to track the original thirteen women on pretrial remand until they were convicted or acquitted, and to follow those convicted until sentence and beyond. Given the time lag for different stages in the remand process, it was decided that the most efficient and effective research method would be a form of staggered cohort sampling – selecting overlapping samples rather than following one sample chronologically.

To ensure that, whenever possible, cases were tracked through successive stages of remand, the women in Sample A were selected first and the initial information collected on them in order to allow the maximum possible time to elapse before it was necessary to select Sample B. In the event, four of the women in Sample A did continue into Sample B, with an additional nine new women selected on presentence remand, to make a total of 13 women for this sample. Samples A and B therefore partly overlapped.

Similarly, before Sample C was selected, five women already in the remand samples had passed to the sentence stage and were therefore included in this sample: one had been in pretrial custody only and in Sample A; two had been in custody only after conviction and in Sample B; and two had been on remand in custody throughout and therefore in both Samples A and B. Three more sentenced women were selected to bring Sample C to a total of eight; two had been released on bail after initial periods of pretrial custody occurring before the research began, while the last, by way of contrast, had been on bail until sentence. The samples therefore included some women who were tracked throughout the remand stages to sentence and others whose experience illustrated the problems facing and posed by women at particular points in the remand process.

The samples were designed to provide descriptive examples, their size precluding statistical analysis. The sampling method involved observing all cases passing through Reception (the initial entry process into Holloway) and Reception Board (the interview session on the morning following entry) and identifying the unconvicted remands for selection in Sample A. Care was taken to achieve a distribution of alleged offences reflecting the general pattern for this category of prisoner, as revealed in successive population profiles compiled by Holloway's Psychology Department. A similar strategy was adopted for selection of the additional cases required for Sample B.

For all the sample cases, the Holloway cards and files were examined to obtain background information. Observation at Reception and Reception Board provided a wealth of information at successive stages about each individual. These observations were backed up by individual and group discussion with members of staff at different levels who worked with the women in the samples. These included prison officers and governor grades, probation officers, nursing staff and other individuals involved in particular cases.

Each woman prisoner in the samples was interviewed repeatedly at successive points in her passage through Holloway, beginning with interviews as soon as possible after entry. Subsequent interviews were valuable in enabling the re-examination of first impressions as well as eliciting their experiences of a prolonged stay. The interviews began with routine questions about straightforward details, confirming or elaborating data already on file, and moved on to more personal and potentially stressful questions. The interviews proceeded from a relatively structured to an openended format, allowing for the discussion to move where the individual prisoner wished. On the strict condition of anonymity, the interviews were far-ranging and often intense. It was clear that many of the women felt an urgent need to talk about their situation and problems.

The interviews elicited information about the women's personal histories, including their parental home, their relationships with spouses or co-habitees, their children, their education and work experiences, their health and their past involvement with the criminal justice system. This served as a backcloth to the information on their present alleged or proved offence(s), current experience in their ongoing case, their needs and difficulties within the prison and the effect on their lives on the outside.

To supplement the in-depth investigation of the samples and to define its relevance to the Holloway remand population as a whole, a snapshot of the general characteristics of the total remand population was taken. All the prison cards for every woman on remand on a particular day in early 1985 were examined for remand status, details of age, offence charged, previous record, marital status, children, employment and living arrangements. The social information was not always routinely available on the records and there is some question as to the consistency with which the answers were recorded by prison staff, but they are the only general information available to the prison system. The social data on the official files were derived mainly from the women prisoners themselves without verification. The information in which the prison is more interested – offence, dates of arrest and appearances, past convictions and court decisions – appeared to be collected more systematically.

This exercise enabled the social characteristics of the samples to be compared with those of the remand population as a whole, to the extent permitted by the quality of the official records. This indicated that the domestic and other situations described by women in the samples were not uncommon among female remand prisoners generally.

Plan of the Report

Chapter One draws together and presents a brief overview of the literature and information available about women in the criminal justice system, to place the subsequent examination of women in prison in context. It deals successively with the main issues concerning women's involvement in crime: reporting of female crime, decisions regarding the prosecution of women, the treatment of females in the court process and women's imprisonment.

Chapter Two draws on the original research to illustrate and explain the needs and problems which women remanded in custody experience in relation to their ongoing court cases. It examines the degree to which the prison system addresses these needs and problems and the civil liberties implications of this situation.

Chapter Three is concerned with the effect of custodial remand on women prisoners' personal lives both in prison and outside it. It provides examples of how the atmosphere and conditions of prison life punish women held on remand and how the obstacles to access to their lives beyond prison act as an additional punishment.

Chapter Four examines the practical realities of special care in Holloway. It contrasts the planned specialist role of the new Holloway with current provisions and practice in the main specialist care areas – child care and pregnancy, drug dependence and care of the highly disturbed.

Chapter Five draws together the main issues highlighted by the research and discusses the lessons to be learnt from Holloway. It sets out detailed suggestions for practical change, focusing primarily on Holloway, and indicates the broad policy implications for the prison system generally.

Notes
1. Most of the research at Holloway has been conducted through the Directorate of Psychological Services and presented in the form of internal reports in the Home Office DPS Report Series. These studies deal with specialised subjects, such as self-injury, fires, and the mentally abnormal offender. (See C. Stewart, Fires in Holloway: A Survey of All Fires Occurring from February 1977 to November 1980, DPS Report, Series II, No. 120; C. Stewart, Disturbed women in Holloway. Evidence for submission to the Committee on Mentally Abnormal Offenders, 1973; C. Sloan, A Study of Mothers and Infants in Holloway Prison, 1972)

chapter one:
Theories and Facts

This chapter attempts to draw together a brief overview of existing literature and available information on the position of women in the criminal justice system. It aims to highlight current issues concerning women's involvement in crime, in the prosecution process and in the prison system and to put the ensuing research analysis, findings and recommendations in context.

In order to understand what is happening to the women on whom this research is based it is necessary to know more about how women end up in prison and who these women are. Existing literature and official statistics do not contain a great deal that specifically addresses the issues raised by women, who are a numerical minority in the criminal justice system, just as they are in the prison population.

This has important implications for the ways in which women are perceived and handled by the system. Half of the general population is made up of women, yet those known to be in conflict with the criminal law are predominantly men. A tendency has therefore developed for women in the criminal justice system to be seen as exceptions to the male norm.

This chapter begins by tracing the first steps in a woman's path towards prison. It discusses the theories and evidence concerning the reasons why and extent to which women break the criminal laws of this society, examines information available on the incidence of female involvement in crime and reviews the literature on reported crime committed by women and the process of their labelling as criminal.

The ways in which women are handled in the criminal justice system, as they pass through the various sifting stages on the path to sentencing, are explored and finally attention is given to women in the prison system: the nature of the population, the facilities made available and their lives in prison.

Part I: Women and Criminal Behaviour

The extent to which women's behaviour conflicts with the criminal law is uncertain, as is the extent of men's involvement in criminal behaviour; one may only surmise from what is known about

reported criminal behaviour. This gap between actual and reported criminal involvement is important.

In terms of reported criminal behaviour men are so strikingly in
the majority that it is hard to avoid the conclusion that women
actually, as well as reportedly, behave criminally less often than
men. At the time of this research study, 83% of all persons
cautioned for, or found guilty of, indictable offences were men and
only 17% women.[1] There has however been little research into this
stark difference.

It has been argued[2] that on the whole crime is 'peripheral' to
women, in the sense of isolated or incidental behaviour, rather
than behaviour which is supported by a sub-cultural base.

Another explanation of the differences in reported crime for
males and females points to their different tolerance levels for
delinquent behaviour. Research has found that girls are more
likely to condemn delinquency than boys,[3] although it is not clear
whether this difference in attitude reflects a greater readiness on
the part of girls to adhere to parental or societal norms or a
difference in the pressure to adhere exerted upon girls or boys, or
both.

Boys exhibit higher self-reported rates of offending than girls,[4] a
difference perhaps similarly linked to a variation in tolerance of
delinquency, since girls may be more ashamed of admitting their
own delinquent behaviour. Self-reporting is, in itself, an unreliable
basis for theories of offending differences.

The literature on gender bias in patterns of crime reporting is
interesting but limited. Analysis has revealed that victims or
witnesses of crimes are more tolerant of offenders who are of the
same gender as themselves.[5] Therefore unless a higher incidence
of female victims and witnesses is assumed, no evidence exists that
lower offending rates for women are the result of reluctance to
report women offenders.

It is however possible to hypothesise that there is less reported
female crime because of a difference in detection rates. This need
not mean that females are more skilful at evading apprehension. It
is possible that females are less likely to be caught because of a
general expectation that females are rarely involved in criminal
behaviour.

A number of other theories have evolved to explain the existence
of different crime rates for men and women. Shoplifting has been
adduced as proof of the opportunity theory of female criminal
behaviour, which sees criminal behaviour, like other types of
behaviour, as dependent in part on opportunity. Women, it is
argued, have as much opportunity, if not more, than men to
shoplift because they visit shops more frequently.

Unfortunately, the Home Office's Criminal Statistics for Eng-

land and Wales no longer give a breakdown by individu
categories, such as shoplifting, but combine this wi,
property offences under the broader heading 'theft and ha
Whereas previous shoplifting statistics do suggest that fι   ,
favour this offence above all others,[6] these statistics also inuicate
that women do not shoplift more frequently than men.

In 1978, the last year of criminal statistics showing the more
specific offence breakdown, 43,099 men of all ages were proceeded
against for shoplifting, as compared with 38,518 women. If
opportunity were the full explanation of the male/female offender
ratio, one would expect to see a reverse ratio for this offence
instead of the similar rate shown. A recent study demonstrated that
men were more likely to shoplift than women given equal
opportunity.[7] The opportunity theory would therefore appear to
offer only a partial explanation of the difference in male and
female reported crime.

There are a number of other theories based on expectations
women hold about themselves and expectations others hold about
women.[8] These have been developed by Carlen[9] who discusses the
criminal behaviour of individual women as a response to the
limitations and disabilities placed upon them by virtue of their
expected female roles. Carlen provides accounts of women's lives
before and inside prison which illustrate women's deviance as a
reaction to their awareness of a woman's social disadvantage.[10]

Another explanation favoured in recent years stems from a
medical/psychological approach to women's criminality. The building of the new Holloway Prison on a quasi hospital model owes
much to theories of the woman criminal offender as 'sick', labelling
which may be self-fulfilling. Mandaraka-Sheppard[11] notes that
interest in the population of Holloway Prison has led to the
conclusion that women offenders are often 'psychiatrically ill,
mentally disturbed or unstable'.

Not only is the total attributable incidence of criminal behaviour
lower for women than for men, but individual women tend to have
less extensive criminal histories than men. Again it is impossible to
ascertain the extent of actual behaviour, although the small
amount of quantitative information available points to a difference
between men and women. For example, the 1978 Home Office
Criminal Statistics for England and Wales showed that whereas
about 60% of men convicted of offences (excluding motoring
offences) were estimated as having at least one known previous
conviction, only about 32% of women convicted of these offences
were estimated as having at least one known conviction. It must be
remembered that these figures refer only to convicted persons.

Descriptive literature[12] suggests that one aspect of women's
re-offending is the revolving door pattern, with women constantly

returning to prison for relatively minor offences involving, for example, drinking and prostitution. Although this is not the only kind of female recidivism, it does indicate another difference between the involvement of men and women in crime: women appear to be less frequently involved in serious criminal behaviour such as that involving personal violence or property of high monetary value.

Available information is again limited to recorded criminal offences dealt with by the criminal justice system. From the Home Office Criminal Statistics it is clear that women are under-represented among those cautioned or found guilty of indictable offences, and particularly for offences of violence against the person. In 1984 over three quarters of all women found guilty of, or cautioned for, indictable offences were involved with theft and handling.

Figures compiled by the Home Office for 1970 indicate that 90% of indictable offences committed by women concerned property and that the great majority of these involved sums under £5. Half the property offences were from self-service shops, two thirds involving only food.[13]

Whereas it is still true that women tend not to be cautioned for or found guilty of violent offences, there has been a shift in this general pattern with an increase in the incidence of violent offences among young women cautioned or found guilty. This exceeded the general rate of increase in violent offending. The seriousness of violent crime committed by women has, however, been over-emphasised.[14] Available evidence points towards a predominance of non-predatory, non-stranger violence among women offenders with those known to have committed violent crimes tending to harm relatives or friends.[15]

At the other end of the spectrum are those women involved in trivial offences. Labelling women as criminals for prostitution is in itself a controversial matter. Labelling prostitutes but not their customers as criminal is also controversial, since by definition the offence may be considered an illustration of gender bias. If everyone involved in prostitution were equally regarded as an offender, the usual male predominance would prevail. This is not to argue that such an approach makes more sense than removal of the entire phenomenon from the purview of the criminal law.[16]

The present study is concerned with women defendants and offenders. The involvement of women as perpetrators of crime is however numerically insignificant in comparison to their involvement as victims. Certain offences involve female victims almost exclusively and the growing literature on rape and child abuse bears witness to a shift in awareness concerning female victimisation.[17] However, it is still true that most violence is committed by men against men.

All of the foregoing indicates that women are less involved in conflict with the criminal law than men: whether in terms of total number of offences, repeated offending or gravity of the offence.

Part II: Women in the Criminal Justice System

The lesser criminal involvement of women is associated with some evidence of lenient handling of females in the criminal justice system. Whether this differential practice is the cause or effect is not clear.

There is evidence that informally and formally the police exercise their discretion to pursue cases differently when confronted with men and women suspects. This may be surmised from the statistics for cautioning for indictable offences. Out of the total offender population found guilty or cautioned, women show a higher percentage of cautions than men in each age group.[18]

Whether or not this is the result of preferential treatment of women by the police during these first stages of the criminal justice system has not been clearly demonstrated. Relatively few women are known to the system, few have extensive criminal records and few are involved in serious offences. Higher cautioning would be expected for a population exhibiting these characteristics. In addition there may be a 'chivalry' factor at work.[19] One careful study of police responses to women drug suspects[20] suggests that the exercise of discretion to charge varies according to the suspect's reaction. A woman who cried when apprehended or claimed to have been led astray was more likely to be released without charge than if she responded aggressively. This study indicates that women may evoke a lenient response from representatives of the criminal justice system if they conform to expected female stereotypes.

It would be interesting to see if this occurred at different stages of the criminal process. Unfortunately the information available can establish no more than crude patterns of discretionary practice. Official statistics provide only a schematic outline of what happens to men and women in the criminal courts. Here they face some women, not often as police or lawyers, but rather more frequently as lay magistrates, probation officers and administrative court staff. The increase in the number of women justices of the peace[21] means that a woman may more often stand accused before another woman, although she will probably continue to be defended by a man. In the higher courts the paucity of women is more striking, especially on the bench.[22]

As defendants women suffer the disadvantage of inexperience

since they are less frequently exposed as a group to the court process. One of the first studies to highlight the primitive aspects of the process for the defendant eloquently describes the confusion and vulnerability of the woman accused.[23] More recent research into the response of young men and women to the court experience indicates a contrast between boys, who perceived a sympathetic atmosphere, and girls, who felt shame, fear, confusion and pressure to be passive and to plead guilty.[24]

The court process reveals a strange anomaly in the handling of women defendants. The Home Office Prison Statistics for England and Wales (1982) show 'that females remanded in custody were less likely than males to receive a custodial sentence' over the period 1975 to 1982.[25] In 1982 about three quarters of women remanded in custody subsequently received a non-custodial sentence. During the research period the proportion had decreased somewhat to two thirds. However, this still represents a significant difference from the male remand population, half of which subsequently receiving non-custodial sentences.

The remand population received into prisons and remand centres but subsequently given non-custodial sentences totalled 18,600 men and 1,700 women in 1985,[26] a figure that warrants attention. It has been argued[27] that the adjudication process is in effect used as a form of punishment, with conditions for women serving time in pre-trial custody, but unlikely, ultimately, to be sentenced to imprisonment, often being worse than for sentenced offenders. Women on unconvicted remand who are not remanded between conviction and sentence face slightly less likelihood of imprisonment than women first remanded after conviction and before sentence. The chance of a non-custodial sentence is, however, better than even for both groups. The majority of women remanded in custody before conviction or before sentence will not receive a prison sentence.

Why is prison being used in this way for women? A sentence of imprisonment is less frequently used for women than for men.[28] This difference in the use of custodial sentences is to be expected given that men offenders show a greater incidence of past convictions and are more frequently involved in the more serious offences than women. A sophisticated analysis comparing rates of imprisonment while controlling for offence and record has yet to be carried out to answer this question fully.

The community service order, arguably a more constructive sentencing option, is used relatively infrequently for women,[29] probation being a more favoured sentence for women remanded in custody at some stage of the criminal justice process. When they are imposed, prison sentences tend to be shorter for women than for men.[30] It would, however, be important to control for a number of other factors which might affect this statistic before accepting it as evidence of greater leniency towards women.

The prison population of sentenced women has more than doubled over the last fifteen years. The rate at which custodial sentences are imposed may not have increased substantially, but the absolute numbers have been growing rapidly, contrary to the expectations voiced by the Home Office in the early 1970s.[31]

Why are women remanded in prison rather than given bail? Various theories have been advanced to account for the practice of remanding women who will not subsequently be deemed to warrant custodial sentences. Some of these are based on a perception of women offenders as sick or disturbed.[32] This view is partly based on evidence of a high incidence of medical remands for women. It appears that the woman offender is assessed to ascertain whether she is mentally ill, because her offending is regarded as a more startling and exceptional deviation from the norm, even though it may be more trivial in content.

Whether or not the Home Office circular of 1969 advising all courts to obtain a presentence report before sentencing any woman to imprisonment was based on this view is unclear. This has, however, been regarded as a partial explanation for the use of presentence remands for women and it has also been argued that many social inquiry reports could be made whilst the offender is on bail.[33]

Part III: Women in the Prison System

Prison Establishments for Women

When women are remanded in custody or sentenced to prison there are a very limited number of establishments to receive them. With the closure of the open prison at Moor Court in 1982, the options became even more restricted. Ostensibly this closure was because of a definite fall in the female prison population between 1981 and 1982.

At the time of the research women on remand could be sent to one of four places:

	CNA for women (certified normal accommodation)	Approximate Actual Places for women
Low Newton (Durham)	35	50
Pucklechurch (Bristol)	56	90
Risley (Cheshire)	84	120
Holloway (London)	303	190
	(sentenced & remands)	(remands)

Holloway was the only female establishment holding remands and sentenced prisoners and the only remand establishment exclusively for females. The other three centres, Low Newton, Pucklechurch and Risley cater for remands only of both sexes. In 1988 New Hall, formerly a men's prison establishment, re-opened after conversion for women remanded in custody or recently sentenced, in order to relieve the pressure of rising numbers.

During the research period in 1985 there was an agreed total population ceiling of 350 at Holloway; this has since been increased with additional staffing and the opening of new parts of the building, to 479 in 1987. The certified normal accommodation (CNA)[34] stood officially at 415 during the 1986/87 period.[35] At the time of the research Holloway held 40% of all women remands, making up over half of its total population. It was functioning therefore as a major remand facility. The rise in the total female prison population has resulted in a shift in the proportion of remands at Holloway: the sentenced population now outnumbers the remand population.

Through the 1980's the female remand population has tended to outstrip available prison places. The spill-over into police cells was small in 1985, but increased significantly up to 1987, reflecting the rapid overall increase in the use of police cells for remand prisoners. The average number of men and women prisoners in police cells rose from 45 in 1985 to 537 in 1987.[36] Following the re-opening of New Hall as a women's prison establishment there were no women prisoners held in police cells, but the upward trend in the courts' use of custody has reversed this temporary improvement.

Establishments for sentenced women are not numerous. Three closed prisons exist solely for sentenced women: Styal, Bullwood Hall and Cookham Wood; the first two catering for young offenders as well as adults. Holloway holds sentenced as well as remand women and 'H' Wing of Durham Prison, a local prison for men, serves as a top security facility for women. East Sutton Park, Drake Hall and Askham Grange are the only three open prisons for women, the first two holding young offenders as well as adults. New Hall was recently converted for use as a women's local prison and youth custody centre.

In 1985 there was a total CNA of 1,274 places in women's prisons, of which only 456 were open places, for an actual total of about 1,600 women. Open places were under-used despite indications of overcrowding in closed establishments. The trend has been towards a greater proportion of the female prison population being held in secure facilities. This phenomenon has occurred rather than reclassifying women so as to spread the population as their needs dictate and is noteworthy when one considers the relative lack of violence in women's offence patterns and of extensive serious prior convictions.

The present situation differs markedly from expectations voiced by the Home Office in 1970:

'It may well be that, as the end of the century draws nearer, penological progress will result in even fewer or no women at all being given prison sentences.'[37]

Indeed the basic assumption behind the design for the new Holloway was that a shrinking women offender population committing serious enough crimes to justify sentences of imprisonment would leave only a select female prison population made up chiefly of those in need of therapy.[38] The confluence of the dual notions that women prisoners are mentally ill or disturbed and that women's prisons should provide therapy has been carefully traced from early theories of biological/psychological deficiencies in women offenders to the more recent characterisation of women offenders as mad or bad.[39]

At Holloway the nineteenth century radial stronghold design was replaced in the 1970s by a medically oriented model for a multi-functional establishment with small therapeutic units: the official view at the time was that this new Holloway would be the equivalent of a secure hospital.[40] The architectural result is a conglomeration of units, shut off from each other and strung out along an endless route of walkways.

The design does not favour efficient security, although it was intended to provide a secure unit for serious women offenders other than the small group classified as highest security risks and housed in the sophisticated control conditions of H Wing, Durham Prison. Sightlines are restricted in the new Holloway. The wing staff office in a unit does not command a view of the unit. Corridors bend or turn sharp corners, obstructing vision. From a security standpoint the design is highly labour intensive; staff must be posted at frequent points to maintain visual coverage. For the prisoner the sense of isolation is increased.

The Population of Women Prisoners

Who are the women at Holloway and the other smaller women's establishments? Like their male counterparts, they tend to come from the lower end of the socio-economic scale, with early data on the Holloway population indicating few homeowners.[41] Economic factors have been viewed as the most important motivation for criminal behaviour among samples of women prisoners,[42] a large proportion coming from deprived and disorganised social backgrounds and sharing a common experience of financial difficulties and an inability to find means of livelihood.

A high proportion of women prisoners have experienced disrupted marriages[43] and emotional disturbances or neuroses,[44] but it is not clear to what extent these characteristics are the cause or effect of living in institutions.

A significant proportion, fluctuating between one in four and one in five, is from ethnic minorities or of African or South American origin, due in no small part to the marked effect of longer prison sentences for drug importation on the numbers of non-British nationals in the female prison population.

It is important to reiterate that the majority of women in prison are not accused or convicted of violent offences. Theft, handling, fraud and forgery account for 58% of sentenced women entering prison, violence against the person accounts for only 10%, with burglary and robbery accounting for 6% and 1% respectively. The most common offences are theft or handling, although drug offences are also numerically important. The recurring population of women prisoners charged with drinking offences has recently declined.

Legislative changes in 1981 which made soliciting for prostitution a non-imprisonable offence have had less effect on women's imprisonment than perhaps was intended; research on fines reveals that some magistrates may increase the amounts of fines imposed for these offences, with the result that the same women who previously served time in prison for the substantive offence may now serve time for fine default.[45] A small proportion of the female prison population on any given day is in prison for fine default; they represent a sizeable group in terms of receptions into prison, totalling 1,385 annually at the time of the research, or 29% of the total of 4,733 women received under sentence.[46]

What of the other women who work in the prisons? Evidence to the House of Commons Expenditure Committee Enquiry into Women in the Penal System pointed to staff shortages, the need to work long hours of overtime and the general exhaustion of staff reflected in high sick rates. The Chief Inspector's Report on Holloway (1984) noted the inexperience of staff, 20 still serving their probationary period and another 93 with only one to three years' experience out of a total of 289. It also pointed to the high sickness rate, (on average 30 days of work lost each year per officer).

An internal survey of work stress, conducted by the Holloway Psychology Department in 1984, revealed that staff emphasised the need for more continuity on the wings and more consultation about inmates. This survey indicates the frustration of Holloway staff over physical conditions, long hours and organisation of work.

Difficult women prisoners were mentioned least frequently as a problem, with staff shortages and lack of staff continuity most often mentioned. The survey provides a snapshot of the staff. The majority were under 35 years of age, single, separated or divorced and not cohabiting; despite the relative youth of the group, less than one in ten of the staff had children under 16.

In 1982 the Prison Department reported[47] no difficulty in meeting recruitment targets, but indicated that women officers tended to leave more quickly than men. Whilst the recruitment campaign in 1984 at the time of the research stated the intention of drawing in more people from ethnic minorities, there were and still are few black female prison officers. The nursing staff at Holloway, however, was made up predominantly of black women .

Men prison officers have been employed in women's prisons for a long time. Until recently they worked in areas such as the gate, where personal privacy was less of an issue. Among the management levels the ratio of men to women was conspicuously high. In an effort to overcome staffing problems fourteen senior male officers have been introduced into Holloway in the last year and now work on the wings. This has been described officially as part of a policy of mixed staffing generally and some women prison officers have now been posted in men's establishments. The development is partly a consequence of the Sex Discrimination Act, which enabled women prison officers to argue that their possibilities for promotion were severely limited by the paucity of women's prisons. Whereas the theory behind mixed staffing rests in part at least on the civilising and humanising effect of integrating men and women officers seen in other prison systems,[48] in practice staff shortages and the predominance of men officers in the prison service are more likely to affect the extent to which mixed staffing is introduced across men's establishments as well as in women's establishments.

Lastly there is a small proportion of children living in prison with their mothers. A 1982 survey[49] found 80 mothers eligible to have children in the mother and baby units at Holloway, Styal and Askham Grange; 32 children were actually in such units. The survey provides some interesting statistics on mothers in prison: 22% were first offenders, with the majority never having been in prison before and having cared for their child(ren) prior to arrest.

The survey notes that 122 children under the age of 15 had been living with their mother until her prison sentence and were then transferred into local authority care. Twenty two of these children were eligible for mother and baby units and 13 of the mothers would have liked to have the children in prison with them.

The concept of mother and baby units sits strangely amid the prevailing confusion of philosophies within the prison system. The presence of such units in places like Holloway serves to highlight the multi-faceted dilemma facing women in prison and those who administer the prison system. Should women be accorded different treatment from men as parents; if not, why are there no father and baby units in prison? How do the punitive and rehabilitative approaches to female imprisonment correspond with the provision for children in prison? What assumptions about women and men underlie this curious adjunct to the female prison system?

Life in Prison

There is not a great deal of detailed information about life in English prisons for men or women, partly because of the secrecy which has surrounded the prison system in this country, in contrast to the situation elsewhere, for example in the United States. Nevertheless official sources and authorised research provide fragments of information about what life is like in female prisons, while a slightly more relaxed attitude towards the presence of outside researchers within the prison walls is developing following the recommendations of the Control Review Committee (1984).[50]

The Prison Department's reports show that the type of work available for women in prison differs from men prisoners' work, the orientation for women being towards domestic tasks.

Women prisoners (as well as women staff in prisons such as Holloway) report sick far more frequently than men. The provision of medication occurs far more frequently for women than for men, even allowing for the higher incidence of medication in the female population generally. Official statistics are inadequate in this area since a 'dose' of an individual medication could mean any one of a variety of quantities – from a tablet to be taken three times a day to a single injection effective for a week. Despite such difficulties with the official information, there appears to be strikingly high dosage rates in women's prisons, especially in Holloway.[51] This cannot be explained simply by a higher incidence of women requiring specialist/psychiatric treatment.

The Prison Department in 1980 indicated a shift in expectation from 1970 when it had envisaged a dwindling population of women prisoners requiring primarily specialist help; it now recognised the increasing similarities between the male and female prison populations,[52] as more women were received to serve sentences for violence against the person. The increasing similarities were only relative, since the Prison Department noted the continuing contrast in terms of the predominance of theft offences and fewer previous convictions among women prisoners.

Women are recorded as offending against prison discipline about twice as often as men. Official statistics offer no explanation of this difference. Such research as does exist points to differences in offence reporting, the application of different rules concerning inmate behaviour, and different expectations and responses to the show of aggression by men and women inmates. A recent study[53] demonstrates a greater prevalence of reported misbehaviour among young single women without children and associates this with certain institutional features, particularly a 'negative authority structure', poor inmate/staff relations and staff's age and experience.

It is only recently that this kind of investigative study in prison has been possible in this country,[54] but it is clear that more needs to be known about how women relate to the experience of prison and how they relate to others in prison.

Despite the paucity of research into life in women's prisons, there is a small body of literature which describes the prison experience, mainly from the perspective of former prisoners. The contributions take the form of personal accounts drawn together by common themes of the petty and punitive nature of prison regimes, dislocation from home and disintegration of life on the outside.[55] Audrey Peckham[56] provides a detailed and disturbing picture of conditions in custody and prison ethos, arguing from first-hand experience for the need to focus on the remand prisoner. These accounts have helped to dispel the secrecy and ignorance surrounding the practical realities of prison life and to raise civil liberties questions with respect to women prisoners.

In addition, a number of recent reports about Holloway provide information which is up to date and reliable. Late in 1984 the Chief Inspector of Prisons reported on Holloway.[57] The inspections occurred in early 1984, when building was still in progress, and much of the description is coloured by the disruptive effect of departments' and units' changing accommodation and shifting temporary quarters.

By late 1984, when this study began, the new building programme was advanced and several new units were occupied. Nonetheless the limited range of activities available to prisoners, such as work, education and association, had not significantly improved. Education had played a central role in the medical therapeutic approach favoured in Holloway prior to 1981. At the time of the research, the education department at Holloway consisted of 16 full-time teachers and a part-time budget for 3,000 teaching hours per year. This impressive resource was, however, not in use for much of the research period[58] and it became clear that provision of education depended less on teaching resources than on availability of prison officers to escort women prisoners to classes.

The specialist functions of Holloway, in particular the unit for the highly disturbed, C1, had come under sustained severe criticism from organisations such as NACRO, NCCL and MIND, as well as in the press. At the end of 1984 a question in the House of Lords led to the setting up of a Home Office Project Committee to look into the population of Holloway, its specialist functions and regime. The ensuing report[59] noted that Holloway was operating a 'very reduced regime'.[60] The design of the new buildings was intended to give prisoners maximum freedom within a secure perimeter. Ironically it achieved the opposite effect.

The report made some interesting comments and recommendations concerning staffing policy and the staff-intensive nature of the new Holloway design. It urged the replacement of C1 by a new separate unit and a fresh approach to running the unit. It commented on the need to increase Holloway's population capacity as rebuilding was completed. This last change has occurred, but the new unit for C1 is still in the planning stage. Many of the other recommended changes remain unimplemented.

Gaps in the Literature

This survey of literature and available information has pointed to the paucity of data concerning women in the criminal justice system in general and in the prison system in particular. As a small numerical minority, women have tended to be overlooked. When attention is focused on them, the tendency is to view them almost as freaks of nature. The deviance of women seems to be recorded as more profound and disturbing than the more frequent deviance of men.

Women's social conformity and deviance is a phenomenon worthy of study, if for no other reason than the adherence by the overwhelming majority to the norms of society. However, instead of provoking dispassionate enquiry, women's criminality tends to elicit irrational responses or at best a lack of coherence between ideas and practice. The history of the new Holloway is a classic example of this.

Notes

1. Home, Office, *Criminal Statistics England and Wales*, 1985.

2. F. Heidensohn, *Women and Crime*. London: Macmillan, 1985.

3. R. Morris, 'Attitudes towards Delinquency' in *British Journal of Criminology*, vol. 5, 1965.

4. M. Gold, *Delinquent Behaviour in an American City*. California: Wadsworth, 1970.

5. D. Steffensmeier & R. Steffensmeier, 'Who reports shoplifters?' in *International Journal of Criminology & Penology.*, vol. 5, 1977.

6. P. Mayhew, 'Crime in a Man's World' in *New Society*, June 1977.

7. A. Buckle & D.P. Farrington, 'An Observational Study of Shop-lifting' in *British Journal of Criminology*, vol. 24, 1984.

8. R. Cloward & L. Ohlin, *Delinquency and Opportunity*. London: Routledge & Kegan Paul, 1961; P. d'Orban, 'Social and Psychiatric Aspects of Crime' in *Medicine, Science and the Law*, July 1972; R.I. Mawby, *Women, Crime and Law Enforcement*. Unpublished paper, Nov. 1977; P. Mayhew, op. cit., 1977.

9. P. Carlen, *Women's Imprisonment*. London: Routledge & Kegan Paul, 1983.

10. P. Carlen, J. Hicks, J. O'Dwyer, Diana Christina & C. Tchaikovsky, *Criminal Women*. Cambridge: Polity Press, 1985.

11. A. Mandaraka-Sheppard, *The Dynamics of Aggression in Women's Prisons in England*. Aldershot: Gower, 1986.

12. F. Heidensohn in S. McConville, *The Use of Imprisonment*. London: Routledge & Kegan Paul, 1975; J. Baldwin and A. Bottoms, *The Urban Criminal*. London: Tavistock Press, 1976.

13. F. Heidensohn in McConville 1975, *op. cit.*.

14. A. Mandaraka-Sheppard, *op. cit.*.

15. F. Heidensohn in McConville 1975, *op. cit.*.

16. S. Edwards, *Female Sexuality and the Law*. Oxford: Martin Robertson, 1981.

17. G. Chambers & A. Millar, *Investigating Sexual Assault*. Edinburgh: HMSO, 1985; R. Hall, *Ask Any Woman: A London Inquiry into Rape and Sexual Assault*. Bristol: Falling Wall, 1985.

18. Home Office, *Criminal Statistics England and Wales*.

19. R. Mawby, *op. cit.*.

20. L.B. DeFleur, 'Biasing Influences on Drug Arrest Records: Implications for Deviance Research' in *American Sociology Review 40*, 1975.

21. F. Heidensohn, 1985, *op. cit.*.

22. *Ibid*.

23. S. Dell, *Silent in Court*. London: Bell, 1971.

24. H. Parker, M. Casburn & D. Turnbull, *Receiving Juvenile Justice*. Oxford: Blackwell, 1981.

25. Tables 2(c) and 2(d).

26. Home Office, *Prison Statistics England and Wales, 1986*.

27. R. Morgan & R. King, *A Taste of Prison*. London: Routledge & Kegan Paul, 1976.

28. F. Heidensohn in McConville, 1977, *op. cit.*.

29. L. Dominelli, *Women in Focus: Community Service Orders and Female Offenders*. Nuffield Foundation, 1984.

30. Home Office, *Prison Statistics England and Wales 1986*, Table 1.6.

31. Home Office, *The Treatment of Women and Girls in Custody*, 1970.

32. L. Bowker, ed. *Women, Crime and Criminal Justice*. New York: Lexington Books, 1978.

33. S. Dell, *op. cit.*.

34. The accommodation in each prison establishment is officially certified for a stated number of prisoners. Most of the Victorian locals, for example, were originally built on the assumption of single cell occupancy, so that their CNA is substantially lower than the actual prisoner population.

35. Home Office, *Report of the Work of the Prison Service*, 1986/87.

36. A breakdown by sex is not routinely available, but on 31 January 1988 there were 25 women out of a total of 758 prisoners in police cells. NACRO, 'Prisoners in Police Cells'. Briefing Paper, 1st August, 1988.

37. Home Office, The Treatment of Women and Girls in Custody, *op. cit.*.

38. R.P. Dobash, R.E. Dobash & S. Gutteridge, *The Imprisonment of Women*. Oxford: Basil Blackwell, 1986.

39. *Ibid.*

40. *Ibid.*

41. C. Gibbs, 'The Effect of the Imprisonment of Women upon their Children' in *British Journal of Criminology*, vol. 11, April 1971.

42. A. Mandaraka-Sheppard, *op. cit.*.

43. A. Bedford, 'Women and Parole' in *Brit. J. Crim.*, vol. 14, April 1974.

44. S. Eysenck & H. Eysenck, 'The Personality of Female Offenders' in *British Journal of Psychiatry*, pp. 693-99, 1973.

45. S. Casale & S. Hillsman, *The Enforcement of Fines as Criminal Sanctions*. New York: Vera Institute of Justice, 1986.

46. Figures for 1985 from Home Office, *Prison Statistics England and Wales*, 1986, Table 1.3.

47. Home Office, *Report of the Prison Department*, 1982.

48. Practice in the Swedish and American federal systems and in some American state systems favours staff integration. The American Correctional Association's Commission on Accreditation for Corrections applies a code of standards including equal opportunity for men and women staff at any prison establishment. (American Correctional Association, *Standards for Adult Correctional Institutions*, 2nd ed., January 1981, Standard 2-4056).

49. K. Nooney, L. Eastwood & I. Ray, *A Census of Mothers in Penal Institutions on 15 March 1982*. DPS Series II, No. 132, 1984.

50. Home Office, *Managing the Long-Term Prison System*. Report of the Control Review Committee, 1984.

51. Official statistics show the dosage rate in Holloway falling from three doses per prisoner per day to one dose per prisoner per day during the 1980's. Home Office, *Prison Statistics England and Wales*, 1986.

52. Home Office, *Report of the Prison Department*, 1980.

53. A. Mandaraka-Sheppard, *op.cit.*.

54. The English literature lacks the breadth of research into female prisoners' responses to imprisonment to be found in the United States. It is impossible to assess the relevance to the English context of phenomena revealed in American research, such as the complex lesbian relationships in prisoner culture (D. Ward & G. Kassebaum, *Women's Prisons*. London: Weidenfeld, 1965) and the patterns of familial role playing by groups of women prisoners (R. Giallombardo, *Society of Women*. New York: Wiley, 1966).

55. U. Padel & P. Stevenson, *Insiders: Women's Experience of Prison*. London: Virago, 1988.

56. A. Peckham, *A Woman in Custody*. London: Fontana, 1985.

57. H.M. Chief Inspector of Prisons, *Report on H.M. Prison Holloway*, 1984.

58. Official inspections carried out at the time recorded a 50% closure during one week of the inspections (Department of Education & Science, *Report by H.M. Inspectors on H.M. Prison Holloway*, 1985).

59. H.M. Prison Service, *Holloway Project Committee Report*, July 1985.

60. *Ibid.*, s. 8.2.

chapter two:

Case Related Problems of Women on Remand

This chapter draws upon the original research data to identify, explain and illustrate the case-related needs and problems confronting and posed by women remanded in custody. It examines the extent to which these are addressed and resolved by the prison system, explores the implications for civil liberties and suggests practical remedies and changes.

The term 'due process' is used throughout this chapter. It is derived from the United States Constitution and embraces all rights and presumptions in favour of an individual involved in the criminal justice process, such as the right to unobstructed access to the courts and the right to be presumed innocent until proven guilty.

In the English context, in the absence of a written constitution or of clear and comprehensive codification of the legal rights of a person before the courts, due process has a complex status. It exists as a result of case law and common law tradition, but does not always consist of legally conferred rights. For example, there is a presumption in favour of bail rather than an absolute right to bail.

In English law an accused or convicted individual 'in spite of his imprisonment, retains all civil rights which are not taken away expressly or by necessary implication'.[1] Among these civil rights are rights with respect to due process.[2]

This chapter deals with different aspects of due process in turn:

> remand status
> legal representation
> bail/ custody issues
> appearance in court
> remand for reports.

In reality these areas of need often overlap considerably and for any one individual represent a complex web of difficulties which intertwine and reinforce each other.

The chapter proceeds from the premise that remand in custody places the prison system under an obligation to address and provide for due process needs and problems. The case examples from the research at Holloway illustrate how custodial institutions are not geared to meet prisoners' rights and how the reality of remand in custody prejudices due process. The removal of women on remand from their homes and local courts restricts their ability to help themselves, by restricting freedom of movement and independent action and by increasing reliance on some, while hampering access to others.

Remand Status

Remand prisoners have a different status from sentenced prisoners and they have a need to assert that distinction. Their continued involvement in a case before the courts entitles them to due process of law.[3]

However, the prison system does not accord priority to these distinctions. In theory the presumption of innocence is a cornerstone of the English legal system, but this theory is not translated into practice. One can conceive of a prison system designed to hold unconvicted persons separately from the convicted and remand prisoners separately from sentenced, but, for a variety of historical and short term economic reasons, the prison system holds the majority of remand prisoners in hybrid establishments catering for a mixture of unconvicted remands, convicted remands and sentenced prisoners.

In such an establishment like Holloway differences of status become blurred. The pressure of numbers does not facilitate the separation of the three population groups. At the time of the research, women in the convicted and unconvicted remand samples shared accommodation and, at times, a woman recently sentenced and awaiting allocation to another prison would share with a woman on remand.

This mixing up of women with different legal status presented problems for staff and prisoners alike. Confusion abounded as to prisoners' status and why women were there. Some staff objected to remand women in the samples being offered a mint or a cigarette:

'They are supposed to be in prison, you know.'

Discussion with staff revealed the difficulties of dealing with a mixed population of women. Most staff perceived that the sentenced women 'deserve to be here'; the position of the women on remand evoked a greater variety of responses. Some staff members stated frankly that particular women on remand 'shouldn't be in here'. Others expressed a more general view that many remands were unnecessary. The discussion turned on the relatively trivial nature of the offence which was almost invariably taken as proved, even for unconvicted remands.

Often a staff member's response was related to the character and background of the individual prisoner, rather than her status. When a woman was exhibiting 'disturbed' behaviour there was frequently consensus among prison officers and nursing staff that Holloway was 'not the right' place for her. The question of status did not appear to be a central concern.

In theory, unconvicted remand prisoners have different entitlements from convicted remands or sentenced prisoners. Unconvicted prisoners are allowed to wear their own clothes (Prison Rule 20), but this distinction is blurred for women in prison by the practice, not acknowledged in the Prison Rules, of permitting all women prisoners to wear their own rather than prison clothes. In reality poverty and dislocation – separation from home – are more likely to determine women's ability to wear their own clothes. The Holloway population wears an odd assortment of personal and prison clothes depending upon availability and fit and not on prisoner status.

Until recently unconvicted remands were allowed to have food brought in by visitors[4] and are entitled to daily visits. In practice dislocation made these privileges meaningless for some women. Indeed, they might well receive fewer visits than sentenced women in Holloway.

Unconvicted remands are not obliged to work but, in the prevailing regime of inactivity and lock-up at the time of the research, some of the women in the samples offered to work as wing cleaners to alleviate the boredom. 'At least I get out of the room'. Again the distinction between the different types of prisoners was lost in the practical realities of daily life in Holloway.

A further factor contributing to the blurring of distinctions was the chaotic and shifting timetable at Holloway. Staff and prisoners were constantly confronted with new faces. Staff would arrive for duty in the morning not knowing their assignment until they consulted the notice board. Lack of continuity was the norm. Staff teams changed constantly, depending inter alia on external demands for escort to court. Prisoners were constantly shifted from one unit to another as they came and went from court. In the juggling to place new arrivals or returning prisoners the legal status of the individual assumed secondary importance.

The ultimate manifestation of the obscuring of distinctions within the Holloway population was the high security restrictions imposed indiscriminately throughout the establishment. The endless series of locked doors between units and the requirement of officer escort for all movement between units was in itself punitive. This level of security was designed to suit the very small minority deemed to be 'high risk' cases. The rest of the prisoner population suffered the effects of this policy regardless of status. Ironically if they were later convicted, sentenced and allocated to other prisons, sample women found themselves in less punitively restrictive security than they had experienced on remand in Holloway.

Much might be improved by setting a higher priority on prisoner status. This might be achieved by reorganising establishments into separate units catering for remands versus sentenced prisoners, where different security levels could operate.

Differences in regime, other than the security dimension, might also be provided in the separate units. In remand units facilities for contact with the outside and activities within the establishment should be tailored to the needs and problems of the remand population. Short term and urgent needs, especially those relating to due process, should be addressed specifically in all aspects of the regime, including information, legal and bail advisory services. It is neither necessary nor advisable for prison establishments to be monolithic in structure or organisation.

Legal Representation

Although there is no right to representation in all circumstances under English law, the need for legal advice exists almost by definition for people remanded in custody because of their right to apply for bail. Remand prisoners also need to consult and obtain information on all aspects of their case , including plea, choice of venue, committal, evidence and a host of other matters. Among the observations on Holloway which the Chief Inspector's 1984 report[5] drew to the attention of the Regional Director was the fact that 'the quality and quantity of general information provided to inmates about their rights, privileges and procedures etc. was inadequate and in need of review and improvement'.[6]

Given solicitors' busy schedules and defendants' resources, communication between lawyers and prisoners is often difficult on the outside; from inside prison it is harder still. The Holloway research demonstrates the many mundane and complex problems relating to representation which face women remanded in custody. To begin with they need advice on how to obtain legal advice and how to pay for it.

Arranging for legal aid often begins at court but may continue in prison, if necessary. The introduction of duty solicitor schemes at many magistrates' courts means that preliminary legal advice on the spot may be available at an early stage, even if the defendant has not yet managed to arrange for legal aid or private representation. When the services of a duty solicitor have been used and the defendant arrives at Holloway without a legal aid grant, the prison is commendably quick to pick up those cases which have slipped past the court administration. All the sample women who required legal aid had been granted legal aid by the second court appearance or had applications for legal aid in progress.

Holloway's ability to identify and respond on this matter appeared to be linked to the special assignment of an officer to the legal aid task. It may also be due to the somewhat mechanical nature of the function. This does not mean that the task is easy. Anyone who has tried to fill out the detailed legal aid application form will realise how difficult it can be to assist someone else to complete it without knowing that person's circumstances. It does not, however, involve the exercise of discretion and is largely a technical matter.

Some of the women in the samples were content with their representation, but more were not. Interviews revealed how organisational factors contributed to this dissatisfaction. The main issue was dislocation, which affects women on remand far more than it does men. In 1985 the Chief Inspector of Prisons stressed how remand dislocation 'penalises prisoners, lawyers and families very severely'.[7] It is important to stress the particular disadvantage to women on remand.

In large urban areas there are usually local prisons serving as remand centres for men. Because the system of local remand prisons does not exist for women, being on remand has a greater dislocating effect on them than men. Dislocation is not uncommon for men and women *sentenced* prisoners, allocated to establishments often scattered around rural England. However, dislocation has important other dimensions for women on remand, who by definition are involved in ongoing court cases.

Nowhere is this more painfully clear than in contacts with lawyers. Dislocation inhibits direct contact between prisoner and lawyer, although under Prison Rule 37 prisoners are entitled to visits from legal advisers. Women in the samples spoke of cancelled and re-scheduled visits from lawyers and the reluctance of their home-based lawyers to come all the way to Holloway.

Prison organisation exacerbates these difficulties. The constant movement of inmates within Holloway renders any appointment system complicated and there were observed instances during the research of protracted delays while an individual woman was located.

Some of the sample women reported seeing solicitors only on the court day in hurried, nervous exchanges. There may be little time before the case is called or afterwards and women in the sample seemed confused about what had happened in court. One woman returning to Holloway and informed of the reduction in her privileges now that she was on pre-sentence rather than on pre-trial remand, exclaimed 'Convicted? I've been convicted?'

There is a potential conflict between a prisoner's need for regular court appearances as a vital lifeline to the outside world and the drain on court and prison resources. The latter has led the Government to favour longer periods between court appearances, by extending adjournments from 8 to 28 days in some circumstances, although reduction of time spent on remand through immediate implementation of speedy trial legislation[8] would achieve a better balance between the interests of the system and the individual.

When lawyers do make the journey to Holloway and succeed in seeing their clients, this may not always take place in interview accommodation, although under Prison Rule 37(1) prison establishments are obliged to afford 'reasonable facilities' for lawyers' visits. Meetings intended to be confidential may have to be held in the dining area or common areas on the wing, because the provision of consultation rooms has proved inadequate for the needs of the large remand population. When the new Holloway was redesigned planners did not foresee the significant rise in the use of custodial remand: between 1976 and 1985 the average prison population of women on pre-trial remand doubled.[9]

If facilities are limited at Holloway they are virtually non-existent in police cells, where several of the women in the research samples spent part of their time on remand. Solicitors reported having nowhere to talk with their clients in private. One spoke of her difficulty in even locating her client. 'There is a central number to ring. I was informed that she was [in the cells] at Highbury but when I got there they said she'd been moved to South Western.' Highbury corner magistrates' court is in North London, whereas South Western magistrates' court is at the southern extreme of London.

The lack of direct contact with lawyers may mean that between court appearances women depend on letters to express their worries and any queries about the legal process. The limits on letters[10] and telephone contact lead them to rely on other prisoners for information. This may be a mixed blessing, for although it may bring comfort and support in some cases, in others it raises the level of anxiety and misunderstanding.

> Carol had written repeatedly to the court to try to have a previous 'fine' lodged, so that it might be written off by her time served in Holloway, as others had done. Carol had written to her lawyer to no effect. After several communications had travelled between herself and the court, an Assistant Governor realised that the court could not lodge the fine because it was in fact a compensation order.

If a woman remanded in custody fails to use effectively the

solicitor's letter granted upon entry into Holloway – and women in the sample reported being confused especially on first entry, forgetting to mention important points in their letter – there may be a long wait before there is another opportunity to sort out the problem. On some observed occasions during the research women applying through the Assistant Governor at the Reception Board on the morning following entry into Holloway were told that there were no writing materials available.

Personal communication is further restricted by the ban on direct use of the telephone. This is not the case in other countries such as the United States, where the prison organisation relies heavily upon the telephone to speed up case-related matters, ease the burden on staff and defuse tension. Access to payphones was introduced in open prisons and open youth custody centres in 1986, but in Holloway the telephone is only used by staff or probation in an emergency, on behalf of women on remand.

The crisis management characterising Holloway at the time of the research – concentration of resources to respond to changing urgent external and internal system demands – added to the difficulties of those seeking advice or help from their lawyers.

> *Josie was convicted and sentenced to imprisonment and arrived in Holloway on a Thursday. She wanted to consult her lawyer about her appeal. While she was still at court she had set up an appointment for the following Tuesday with her lawyer, who was based in London. On Monday the wing staff learned that she was to be transferred to Styal on the following day. The speed of allocation was not unusual at Holloway, where the pressure of numbers required a rapid movement of prisoners. Josie was distraught about not being able to write to her lawyer in time to schedule an appointment before she left. (She was also upset about leaving her son in London; she had no idea where Styal was, and had only been told that the journey from London would take about five hours). The senior officer on her wing arranged for the prison to call her lawyer's office on Monday, but they were unable to reach him. He arrived at Holloway on Tuesday, but Josie was already on her way to Styal. Two weeks later, when interviewed at Styal, Josie expressed her anxiety about seeing her lawyer again.*

Such obstructions to remand prisoners' access to due process through representation may in turn make a difference to the lawyer's ability to present the case and therefore its outcome. Furthermore, lack of contact with lawyers or severe curtailment of access may produce delays in the court process, which in turn affect the prison population. It is therefore in the interest of the prison system to facilitate legal representation. A system so beset by overcrowding has compelling cause to expedite cases on remand by removing obstacles to communications, particularly when those obstacles are an obvious source of tension within the prisons.

General policy concerning the organisation of prisons for women needs to be reconsidered, taking account of the special disadvantage women on remand suffer from dislocation. It may not be economically viable to run separate local prisons for women, as there now are for men, because the total absolute numbers are so much smaller for women. However, women on remand should not suffer significant disadvantage because of this.

An alternative, recently reiterated by the Howard League,[11] of separate female sections within existing male prison establishments requires careful re-examination, with due attention to the safeguards necessary to counteract the risks of mixed prisons. The danger of sexual exploitation and the claustrophobic effect of extremely small wings for women prisoners are two of the disadvantages which must be weighed against the distress and damage caused by dislocation. This is a question on which emotions run high. There has as yet been no detailed and dispassionate analysis of the practical and political implications of these two less than ideal options.

An immediate practical remedy for the difficulties of communications with legal representatives might be the establishment of a duty solicitor scheme or legal advice centre within the prison. Also, as many women on remand have similar needs for routine and basic information about the court process, a written or taped information service might go some way to alleviate the more common misconceptions and afford general assistance.

More sophisticated back-up help might be provided by making advisers from the duty solicitor scheme or legal advice centre available for on the spot consultation at regular times. Although advice would come from a pool of lawyers and legal advisers rather than a personal legal representative, there is already a good deal of lack of continuity of representation in the criminal process. On balance it is arguably more beneficial to have worrying questions dealt with by someone else at the prison, than for problems to remain unaddressed for long periods. The greatest benefit would accrue if this service were available immediately upon entry in prison.

Arrangements for prisoners writing to lawyers would be improved by small practical changes. For example, writing materials might be made readily available at entry into prison and thereafter and the laborious procedure of applications for letters through assistant governors circumvented.

However, the most obvious and straightforward method of improving communications would be direct telephone access. Experience with this method elsewhere has proved overwhelmingly positive. The due process benefits, both material and psychological, are manifest: direct personal communications, reduction of time lags, in short more effective representation. In addition there is a cogent practical argument: telephone access to legal representatives relieves prison staff of the time-consuming role as go-between and of the accompanying displaced aggression when communications fail.

Bail / Custody

Women remanded in custody fall into two groups:

those granted conditional bail by the court but unable to meet the conditions; and
those remanded in custody without conditional bail.

The first group needs to find ways of meeting their bail conditions or to apply for changed bail conditions; the straight remands need to apply or re-apply for bail.

In the research samples women in both groups exhibited marked confusion about bail. The position in law was not a simple one and different courts chose to interpret differently the *Nottingham Justices* case,[12] which appeared to limit defendants to three successive applications for bail, and then only if the circumstances had changed since the last application. Some courts did not count bail requests at the first appearance as one of the three applications, while others did, and there was wide variation in practice centring upon the question of what constitutes changed circumstances.[13] Since lawyers and magistrates differed on these issues it is hardly surprising that defendants were confused.

Controversy over the *Nottingham Justices* case and the practice of denying defendants the opportunity to re-present the facts after an initial denial of bail led to pressure to change the law. In a recent House of Lords debate on the Criminal Justice Bill, the Minister agreed to an amendment to allow the defendant to 'support an application for bail with any argument as to fact or law that he desires (whether or not he has advanced that argument previously) at subsequent hearings.'[14] This goes some way to improve the defendant's position, although it remains to be seen whether in practice magistrates and judges will be more ready to grant bail when their colleagues have previously refused it.

The notion that defendants have a limited number of opportunities to apply for bail may lead lawyers to delay bail applications until circumstances are most favourable, even though this means delays and longer time in custody.

It took Yola two weeks to meet bail, because her lawyer waited for her reappearance in court to talk to her about reapplying and then waited until the next court appearance, by which time he had made the necessary arrangements for bail conditions (confirmed residence at a relative's house). It is arguable that if he had not had to come from Norfolk to Holloway to see Yola, he might have speeded up the process by direct contact.

Delays in communications inside the prison, as well as dislocation, resulted in some women in the sample waiting through repeated remands while arrangements to meet bail conditions were made.

Passing through Reception Board on her third successive remand Melanie mentioned to the Assistant Governor(AG): 'I wanted to see Probation last time, but I didn't get to see anyone.'

The AG checked her file and asked what the problem was. Melanie: 'They were going to get me into a bail hostel.'

AG consulting the file: 'That was ages ago. I'll put "urgent" on it.'

When Melanie had left, the AG commented that she had been through Reception Board three weeks before and had indeed made an application to see the Probation Department concerning her bail conditions. The AG made it clear that, while this lapse was deplorable, it was not uncommon. Apparently women did fall through the gaps in the system.

Where bail conditions are to be met, communications with the outside are of crucial importance. Family and friends might act as sureties or help to find acceptable accommodation. However, communications with inmates are even more difficult for a person who is not their legal representative. Unconvicted women are allowed one 15 minute visit from up to three adults and children every day; convicted women are allowed one 30 minute visit once every 28 days, although this usually occurs once every two weeks. In practice the long journey, cost and waiting time often make visits unfeasible. In the absence of telephone access, letters become a main form of communication for family and friends, as for legal representatives.

Without direct contact through visits from lawyers or others, the problems of arranging bail may be compounded by misinformation and misunderstanding. One woman spent a week in Holloway unnecessarily because she did not understand her bail conditions:

Jean's brother eventually found the £1,600 needed for bail. Initially he had brought documentation to court showing that he had £1,000 in his deposit account. Apparently no one had explained adequately to him that he could sign for the remaining £600, on the basis of his other assets. He had the impression that he had to produce the total in cash. Jean spent a week in Holloway until this was clarified at the next court appearance.

Straight remands in custody faced similar problems of communication as they tried to apply or re-apply for bail. Although this study is not directly concerned with the court decision-making process, the sample women's perceptions of that process impinged on their actions in relation to bail while in Holloway.

They had initially been judged unsuitable for bail. In law this must be for one of three reasons: likelihood of offending, of absconding or of interfering with witnesses while on bail. Since most women are accused of non-violent and less serious offences, the danger to the public of their offending on bail is minimal.

The risk of a defendant on bail failing to appear is linked to his/her ties with the community.[15] Holloway records[16] indicated that a majority of unconvicted remands had children. The majority of women in the samples had dependent children. In some cases reports indicated that the children were in their care, while in others there was no indication; in two cases the children were reportedly in care of the local authority, but visited regularly by the mother. On the basis of these personal ties the women seemed unlikely to disappear on bail.

From the research it appeared that some women felt they had been remanded in custody not because of any danger to the public, nor because they were likely to abscond, offend or interfere with witnesses, but because of their domestic circumstances. In most instances the straight remands in the samples had 'unsuitable' accommodation – a rental shared with a friend or council accommodation not in the woman's name. A prime need therefore was to arrange for an alternative. From inside prison, cut off by distance and limits on access, that task was often not achieved. Only two straight remands in the samples applied successfully for bail from Holloway.

The result is that women accused of non-violent offences remain for considerable periods in custody. The implication is that some of the women remanded in Holloway need not have been there and this situation cannot be justified. The mere fact of being in custody may adversely affect a woman's prospects when her case is eventually heard, increasing the likelihood (all other things being equal) of a guilty plea, a conviction and a prison sentence.[17] It is nonsensical to burden a prison system already bursting at the seams with prisoners who have been granted bail but end up in prison for virtually mechanical reasons.

The examples from the research demonstrate a lack of communications; but they also reveal a more fundamental flaw. There is no one to screen women on remand in a systematic way to ensure that bail information is received and understood, in order to counteract the difficulties of arranging for bail whilst in custody.

A bail unit inside the prison would be a major improvement. Some local prisons, like Wormwood Scrubs, operate bail units to facilitate arrangements for those on conditional bail. There is no reason why a bail unit within a prison could not deal also with straight remands in custody.

Ideally a bail unit should operate from the point of entry into prison. It need not be a passive reactive mechanism. The women who need it are unlikely to be well informed. A reactive unit serves only those who know and pursue their rights. It is important to insert an automatic sifting device early enough to catch everyone and identify those for whom action is necessary. From the research it is clear that it is not enough to tell everyone that if she has a bail problem she may apply to see a probation officer.

The bail unit would require the designation of staff to cover the post at all times when women enter the prison. This would provide an opportunity for the development and exercise of special professional skills, affording a chance of lateral, if not vertical, promotion for prison staff. In a service with few openings for career enhancement, the bail unit would be a useful management tool. The use of prison officers for legal aid assistance in Holloway is an instance of this kind of practice.

The difficulties surrounding the achievement of bail may not all be solved by making staff available to advise and facilitate, but the presence of a probation officer either throughout the reception period (instead of solely on a nine to five basis as was the case during the research period), or throughout Reception Board, instead of only sporadically, would make a difference.

The availability of hostel places would still present an obstacle to arranging bail. At the time of the research only one hostel in the London area was prepared to consider women with any history of drug dependence, even with evidence that the woman was drug free at the time. Given the size of the drug/alcohol abuse problem among the Holloway population,[18] this represents a serious mismatch of community facilities to their target population.

Court Appearance

The appearance of a defendant or offender when she appears in court may have a significant bearing on the case. Several factors may affect the impression made in court by a woman remanded in custody.

Once again a major problem is the potentially damaging effect of dislocation. Few male prisoners on remand are subjected to the wear and tear of travelling the long distances to court faced by many women at Holloway. The journey from Holloway to Southampton in early morning traffic is scarcely relaxing, yet women in the samples undertook that and similar journeys many times. Prisoners and prison staff on escort confirmed that women arrived tired and in disarray after an early wake up call and hours on the road. Few people would feel or look at their best under these circumstances.

Dislocation adds to the tension of the court appearance, by a frantic concentration of expectation on the brief direct contact with lawyers, family and friends. Into the long day is packed all the stored up business of persons displaced and cut off from their former life. It is a recipe for disappointment.

It was not uncommon for women returning to Holloway to report that they had forgotten to say to their lawyers half the points about which they had been worrying for days or weeks. In the heat of the court day the process of communication has its own momentum; the woman is looking out for a relative or has one ear listening for the arrival of a child. Later after the case has been called, she may be confused as to what actually happened, why her lawyer did not say what she thought he would say, and why the case was adjourned again.

Dislocation presents the prison system too with a major problem, in its obligation to deliver remand women for court appearances. The escort costs for women travelling back and forth to courts many miles from Holloway are high – prison officers are absent from the prison for very long periods on costly overtime – and there are many practical difficulties. Women coming from the London courts must be escorted back to Holloway by 6.00 p.m. and those coming from more distant courts by 7.00 p.m. If they arrive later, they will be 'locked out' – turned away at the gate and escorted to custody in police cells at one of the larger magistrates' courts in the London area.

> Celia described how the car coming from a distant court got lost and arrived at 8.00 p.m. at Holloway. 'They phoned from the gate to see if Highbury would take me . . . Then we got lost and they took me to Highbury Vale. They thought it was the police station but it's the court. They weren't local. They were from Southend because that's where my case is.'
>
> Celia and her escorts seem to have felt equally baffled and misused by the system. 'They said "If they don't accept you at Highbury Corner, we'll get you some fish and chips on the way back to Southend."' Celia was taken eventually in at the Highbury Corner magistrates' court holding cells. 'I didn't eat. I didn't even think of it. I was just too tired.'

During their many weeks on remand in custody three women in the research samples spent an entire adjournment period (three weeks for reports or 28 days awaiting a trial date) in police cells between court appearances. There the facilities for exercise, fresh air, bathing and keeping clothes clean and in a reasonable state were severely limited. One of the magistrates' courts holding centres had only one hand-held shower for the women on remand, who were often detained more than ten at a time. Cells were shared, sometimes between four women, with room barely to lie down on wooden benches or mattresses on the floor. Not surprisingly women held under these conditions appear in court in a general state of tiredness and dishevelment, often with lank hair and creased clothes, stale from continued use and close proximity to others.

This external appearance may be compounded by signs of distress. Remand in police cells is a palpably upsetting experience. When women arrive in court after such an experience the magistrates are not informed of the fact, any more than they are informed of the miles travelled in the early hours of the morning to reach court from Holloway.

Yet these factors may tell against the woman at the court appearance. Traditional female stereotypes, involving neat appearance and hygiene, not to mention conventional notions of attractiveness, may underlie judgements about a woman's ability to cope on bail, or even about her integrity. The history of women's imprisonment testifies to the operation of such norms.[19]

The 1983 commitment by Leon Brittan, the then Home Secretary, to eliminate remands in police cells has been honoured mainly in the breach. In 1989 women and men prisoners still spill over into police custody and will probably continue to do so, given the current state of overcrowding in prison establishments and the continued trend towards greater use of custodial remands.

In the longer term any guarantee of permanent elimination of female remands in police cells requires a much more basic reappraisal of the way in which courts decide to remand women in custody and a rethinking of whether this makes sense in terms of the low risk to the public versus the high cost to the public and to the individual women involved.

Practical steps might be taken to relieve the worst of the immediate difficulties: improved hygiene facilities, both at the prison and at the court, as well as improved arrangements for meetings at court. These mechanical solutions would make conditions somewhat less intolerable, but would not solve the fundamental problem of the way in which custody for women is organised. Until that question is systematically readdressed due process for women on remand will be adversely affected in such seemingly mundane, but potentially vital, matters as their appearance in court.

Remand for Reports

Most of the women remanded for reports in the research samples had already been convicted. One was in Holloway pending medical evaluation to see if she was fit to enter a plea. The others were remanded in custody for social enquiry reports, a third with medical reports also requested. These women, although convicted, continued to have due process needs because the reports would have a bearing on the case outcome, and more particularly whether they would be sentenced to imprisonment or some other penalty.

The problems of report preparation for women remanded in Holloway are many. Since they come from far-flung areas of the country, their local probation officers, some already in contact with them through a previous case and others needing to make first contact for a possible probation order on the current case, are often not in routine contact with the probation department at Holloway. The liaison proceeds slowly. Similarly communications with the local G.P. may be time-consuming and laborious, in part because of dislocation and in part because of bureaucratic red tape. The mechanics may break down to the disadvantage of the individual prisoner.

> *Jenny, originally remanded on bail but remanded in custody after conviction for reports, seemed totally unaware of the reason for her being in Holloway, although this was apparent from her file. Nobody contacted her at Holloway concerning a social enquiry report during the three weeks over Christmas when she was there. At court in January it became clear that no report had been arranged and she was remanded on bail for a further three weeks. The three weeks in Holloway had been 'for nothing' in her own words.*

Jenny did not abscond when placed on bail again. The report was eventually prepared while she was at liberty. This prompts the question of why she was not remanded on bail at the outset. Was this an example of remand in custody as a form of short penalty prior to sentence? Certainly the court judged that she should not spend further time in Holloway either for her report or for her eventual sentence of a fine and a conditional discharge.

Like all those remanded in custody women remanded for reports have a due process need for speedy handling of their cases. The official statistics show that women remanded before sentence generally have a shorter wait than unconvicted remands. Normally reports appeared to be prepared within three weeks during the research period, and this continues to be cited as the convention, but there were periodic slip-ups resulting in longer custody.

> *May was remanded in custody for medical and presentence reports, but when three weeks later she appeared in court for sentence, 'They forgot to give the reports to the escorts'. May came back to Holloway for another week and was finally released on the day of her sentence in court; she was sentenced to one month's imprisonment, already served.*

While dislocation might lie at the root of delays and omissions in the reporting process, the prevailing confusion of daily life in Holloway seemed to be a contributing factor, with its constant movement of prisoners and staff. Moreover, the quality of daily life in Holloway was not conducive to a prisoner's making a good impression for her reports, as may be true of life on remand in custody generally.

As the chief diagnostic / assessment centre for women in England and Wales, Holloway sees a large number of women remanded for medical reports. At the time of the research the majority was pronounced not in need of medical placement and subsequently given a non-custodial sentence. Whether this majority would have been greater if the women had been assessed at liberty is impossible to know.

While in Holloway they were processed through C1 Unit, originally designed as a therapeutic unit for the severely disturbed sentenced prisoner, but in 1985 operating predominantly as a reporting unit for remands. The conditions of strict confinement and inactivity prevailing on C1 are discussed in greater detail in Chapter Four. Arguably those conditions in themselves prevented prisoners making an adequate response as reports were prepared about them which would have a bearing on the disposition of their case in court.

Certain practical amendments to the present process of report preparation might help to alleviate the delays. Improved liaison between the prison and local probation departments and early contact with the remand prisoner are important. There is no reason why the three week period should be sacred. The research found that often the report meeting occurred towards the end of the three week period, so that the writing up time was relatively short. It ought to be possible to reduce the three week period by more efficient scheduling.

Ultimately, however, the best hope of improvement must lie in finding ways of preparing reports outside the prison system. More attention is needed to the provision of hostel accommodation in cases where the home is judged unsuitable. Finally there must be much clearer thinking about the justification for report remands in custody, particularly for individuals previously on unconvicted remand on bail. Does that same individual suddenly pose a much greater danger to the public or present a greater likelihood of absconding ; is post conviction custody intended as a form of short penalty (arguably it has that effect); or does custodial remand for reports arise from administrative convenience, as the court gives priority to professional rather than due process needs?

This chapter has described how the prison system currently fails to come to terms with the due process and other case-related needs of women remanded in custody. Ultimately the fundamental remedy for the existing situation would require rethinking the way in which the prison system is organised. There is a strong case for separate establishments to hold remand or sentenced prisoners,[20] so that the special status of remand prisoners and their due process requirements may be accorded priority.

Previous attempts in this country to hold remand prisoners separately have failed to break away from the traditional prison mould. Moreover, the establishments catering exclusively for remand prisoners are to date few in number and tend, therefore, to concentrate the remand population far from home. Dislocation is not, however, an inherent characteristic of separate remand centres, although it has become associated with the concept through historical example. Local prisons, which currently cater for many remand prisoners, entail far less dislocation than remand centres such as Pucklechurch or Risley.

A more systematic reorganisation would divide the prison system into two parallel groups of establishments catering separately for remand and sentenced prisoners and providing different regimes reflecting the different rights and needs of remand versus sentenced prisoners.

Chapter Three turns to an examination of remand prisoners' needs and problems in relation to their personal lives on the outside and to their rights as private citizens.

Notes

1. Lord Wilberforce in the case of *Raymond v. Honey* [1982] 1 All E.R. 756.

2. Lord Bridge refined Lord Wilberforce's statement concerning the retention of a prisoner's civil rights, stressing 'in particular his right of unimpeded access to the courts.' *Leech v. Dep. Gov. Parkhurst* [1988] 2 WLR 290.

3. Sentenced prisoners also continue to have due process rights with respect to their appeal and, of course, retain the right of every citizen to due process with regard to a new case.

4. In 1988 this privilege was rescinded on the grounds that food brought into prison facilitates the smuggling of contraband and excessive staff time is involved in searching for contraband.

5. H.M. Chief Inspector of Prisons, *Report on H.M. Prison Holloway*, November, 1984.

6. *Ibid.*, Appendix 4, p. 40, s. 14.

7. H.M. Chief Inspector of Prisons, *Annual Report*, 1985, p. 4, s. 2.06.

8. The Prosecution of Offences Act 1983 established the power to set time limits for trial. These have been introduced in some parts of the country and are due to come into force throughout England and Wales by the end of 1990.

9. Home Office, *Prison Statistics England and Wales*, 1986, Table 2(a).

10. Under Prison Rule 37A a remand prisoner is entitled to communicate with her legal representative without censorship and shall be provided on request with the necessary materials. The entitlement to other letters is restricted: two postage paid letters per week for unconvicted prisoners and extra letters with postage paid out of private cash; for convicted remands the allowance is one postage paid letter per week and at least one other, the postage for which must be earned within the prison.

11. The Baroness Seear & Elaine Player, *Women in the Penal System*, Howard League for Penal Reform, 1986, pp. 14-15.

12. *R. v. Nottingham Justices*, ex parte Davies [1980] 2 All E.R. 775.

13. B. Brink & C. Stone, 'Defendants who do not ask for bail' in *Criminal Law Review*, March 1988.

14. Clause 146, *Criminal Justice Bill [Lords]*, Report Stage, 28 June 1988.

15. The Manhattan Bail Project, an early experiment by the Vera Institute of Justice in New York, to develop a system of assessing links with the community, became the model for bail projects across the United States and was influential in the pilot bail project in London in 1975.

16. The information on the prison file card for each woman was not always complete, but where it existed it showed more than half the women with children.

17. A.K. Bottomley, *Decisions in the Penal Process*. Martin Robertson, 1973, pp. 88-93.

18. Drug charges made up the second largest offence group in the Holloway remand population, accounting for 22% of all unconvicted remands. Only theft charges ranked higher, accounting for 29% of all unconvicted remands, but this charge probably masked a large number of drug related offences, to judge from the sample theft cases.

19. R.P. Dobash, R.E. Dobash & S. Gutteridge, *The Imprisonment of Women*, Basil Blackwell, 1986.

20. The argument has been recently stated by Lord Windlesham. 'Punishment and Prevention: The Inappropriate Prisoner' in *Criminal Law Review*, March 1988.

chapter three:

Personal Needs and Problems of Women on Remand

This chapter is concerned with women on remand as individuals with a personal life to lead both in prison and outside it. It examines and assesses whether or how their personal needs on remand are addressed by the prison organisation and explores the implications for civil liberties and the human dignity of those held in custody. The discussion deals with the following aspects of life in prison, concluding with suggestions for possible remedies;-

- prison conditions
- information
- relationships in prison
- links with the outside

Conditions in Prison

Many different factors contribute to conditions in prison. Some key areas were highlighted in the research and serve to illuminate what day to day life can be like for women on remand and how many problems have systemic origins.

The physical surroundings, their layout and the equipment provide the concrete setting, while the behaviour of people within them creates the regime of prison life. Different prisons have their own distinctive style and atmosphere: the product of the established norms and expectations that grow up in institutions closed and isolated from outside influence.

This discussion of prison conditions looks both at the tangible aspects of prison life in Holloway – with hygiene and clothing as illustrations – and the less tangible side – activities and the timetable of 'locking-up'. The requirements for life in prison are contrasted with the operational 'rules' in order to demonstrate the gap between ideal and practice.

(a) Hygiene

The research documented many instances of material deprivation. Even in a modern prison like Holloway, conditions of hygiene may be far from satisfactory. The physical plant appears adequate: cells normally have sinks and lavatories and there are additional facilities outside the cells (such as showers or baths or extra washbasins). However, excessive lock-up leads to lack of access to these facilities. The women generally had one bath a week and, in practice, one cell sink might be shared by several women for a variety of needs.

> *Ellen, a Muslem, needed to wash thoroughly each day according to her religion. Because she was small and slight she could climb into the sink in the dormitory which she shared with three others.*

> *Anne pointed out: 'Not all the girls are as clean as others. Some don't clean the sink properly, where we have to wash our dishes'.*

Since women spent almost all day locked up in cells, they were obliged to wash themselves, their underwear, small items of clothing, cups and other items in the same shared sink. The overall ratio of sinks and baths to inmates may look reasonable on paper. What militated against a higher standard of hygiene was not the standard of equipment but the way in which it was used.

Although hygiene conditions in Holloway are not ideal, they compare favourably with those in many local prisons where men on remand are subjected to the daily degradation of slopping out because of the lack of integral sanitation. Holloway conditions compare well, too, with the conditions in police cells experienced by several women in the samples where the sleeping arrangements often consisted of a mattress on the floor or bench with a plastic covered pillow and no sheets. Sophia noted: 'It was very cold, but the blanket had been used. It was full of stains.' She covered herself with her cardigan and coat.

(b) Clothing

Some forms of deprivation, such as inadequate clothing, caused considerable distress.

> *At Reception Board one young woman with a skirt split from waist to thigh because of a defective zip asked for an appointment with WRVS[1] for additional clothes.*

> *Rose complained bitterly that she had stood no chance of impressing the court favourably, because she had only the tattered jeans in which she had been arrested. She had been unable to wash them because they took*

*too long to dry on the radiator for her to wash them overnight and she
had no change of clothes.*

One form of deprivation may lead to another in the daily life of a
prison:

*Kit did not go outside for two weeks because she only had slippers to
wear. When she came into Holloway her boots were taken away from
her because they had stiletto heels and might be dangerous. At
Reception Board she applied to WRVS to obtain some shoes, because
she had no one to visit her and bring shoes from home. When she saw
WRVS after a fortnight, she had been recorded through an
administrative error as requiring a skirt, so they gave her a skirt. 'They
wouldn't give me shoes. I went down for exercise and they sent me back
because of me slippers.'*

*Kit put in a Governor's Application about her footwear, but it had
not been resolved after three weeks. 'I've been on exercise twice. I
borrowed another girl's boots. She wasn't going.' Borrowing is treated
as an offence against good order and discipline in the prison, but Kit
was not charged when she told the prison officer what she was doing.
The officer turned a blind eye.*

It was lucky for Kit that she had the co-operation of this prison
officer, but the question remains as to whether a prisoner's
exercise, a legal requirement, should depend upon the goodwill of
individual officers in bending the unwritten 'rules' of prison life.

(c) Exercise and Fresh Air
Common sense dictates that exercise, including time in the fresh
air when weather permits, is an important need for persons held in
prison. Under Prison Rule 27 all prisoners, whether remanded or
sentenced, are entitled to 'exercise in the open air for not less than
one hour in all each day'. Circular Instruction 2/1966 has reduced
the daily exercise requirement to half an hour in some prison
establishments.

During the research it became clear that outdoor exercise, a walk
in the open air of the grounds of Holloway, did not happen every
day for all women on remand. When it did happen, weather
permitting, it often involved ten to fifteen minutes outside, the
entire exercise period being calculated from the time of unlocking
until a woman was locked up again. The long distances involved in
getting back and forth in Holloway drastically reduced the effective
time out of doors. 'One time I had ten minutes. After that I started
timing it, to get my fifteen minutes.'

The logistics of exercise appeared to run counter to the routine
functioning of the prison.

One Wednesday afternoon Tess reported in interview that she had not been out for exercise since Saturday afternoon. The weather had been cool, but it had rained only once, on Sunday. On Monday there was no exercise, the stated reason being staff shortages. On Tuesday Tess had gone to court and so had missed exercise; she had not been outside that day apart from walking to the escort vehicle and from it to the court house. On Wednesday exercise had taken place in the morning while Tess was waiting for Reception Board, the prison interview procedure following re-entry into Holloway. In the afternoon she had missed going outside because she was in the process of transferring from the Reception Wing to a more permanent wing in the prison.

Staff on the wing were not able to confirm or deny this set of events because the lack of continuity of personnel meant that no one staff member had been in contact with Tess throughout or for a substantial part of this period. There were no records on the exercise actually received by individual prisoners on the wing. Staff however were prepared to confirm that this account of events might well have been accurate.

The situation for women held on remand in police cells was worse since there was no provision at all for exercise, although women reported that occasionally they were taken out of the cells for a brief walk around the court car park.

(d) Physical Training

As well as exercise in the sense of getting out of doors, prison establishments are intended to offer physical education, i.e. opportunities for sport or other physical activity. The new Holloway boasts a magnificent indoor swimming pool, a large sports hall and remedial gymnasium. By any standards this level of provision is excellent. During the research period these facilities stood empty for most of the time. The empty sports hall, situated as it is on the main route through the prison, was a strong visual reminder to staff passing to go on and off duty of the provision of expensive plant for the new Holloway and the irony of its lack of use. In tangible form it represented the gulf between the ideal and practical reality.

However, since the research was completed a major change has occurred. The sports hall, gym and pool have come into frequent use. Instructors have gone to fetch women from the wings to the gym, circumventing the problem of escort and staff shortages. This has had a spill-over effect on other areas of activity, opening up movement about the prison. It is interesting that no new regulations have been called into play and no change of plant or equipment. The difference lies in the attitudes and actions of key personnel. There is a danger, however, that conditions could easily revert to the lack of exercise and physical training so prevalent in the research period. The research shows that legal requirements were overlooked in practice not merely on odd occasions but on a daily basis.

(e) Education

The prison system is intended to provide education to those prisoners requiring it. There is a statutory obligation to provide full education facilities to prisoners under the school leaving age; ironically for girls under sixteen this means that they must be transferred to a closed prison as no open establishment for female prisoners offers a full school education. At Reception Board, one prison officer commented ruefully as two fifteen year old first offenders were transferred to Bullwood Hall: 'Well, they'll certainly get an education there.'

For older women the educational facilities at Holloway were impressive even at the time of the research and have since improved as the education department has moved into its own area. However, during the research a dispute between management and staff resulted in the cancellation of education, due to the frequent unavailabilty of staff to escort inmates to classes. As the Chief Inspector's Report[2] indicated: 'Even when classes were being held, the number of inmates allowed to attend them at any one time when two discipline officers were on duty was restricted to 40'.

This problem has been solved more recently by greater freedom of movement in Holloway, but the situation at the time of the study illustrates the precarious position of 'non-essential' tasks such as education within the prison organisation. Modern facilities and a large provision of teaching staff provide no guarantee that education will take place.

The women on remand displayed and sometimes articulated a need for education. One woman in the research samples could not read, several were barely functionally literate, several others displayed signs of dyslexia, many had little or no training in a marketable skill and almost all needed education in how to deal with the criminal justice system, the welfare state generally and in particular with the bureaucratic red tape surrounding their detention.

Yet the women on remand were least likely to receive education. The problem was partly organisational. The remand population is transient in the sense of disappearing for odd days to go to court. From the bureaucratic viewpoint the individual is seen as a person on a limited stay and therefore difficult to include in the ongoing educational schedule, which was organised by a laborious process of interview and timetable planning to provide a long term programme. While this might be of value to individuals on sentence and rewarding for the teachers, most of the remand women in the samples wanted education of a more mundane, short term and practical nature, such as how to formulate a clear letter to their lawyer or how to understand their dealings with the DHSS or local council, as well as improving basic literacy and numeracy or acquiring marketable skills.

Many of the women in the samples were not included in the education department's waiting lists, while others did not reach the top of the list. The time taken for them to apply for education, to be seen and evaluated by the department and to be placed on the waiting list often exceeded the period spent in Holloway. Some were briefly transferred on remand to other establishments because of the pressure of numbers at Holloway; when they returned to Holloway, still on remand, they had to begin the application process all over again. Even if education classes had been operating during the research period, many of the sample women would probably not have been able to participate. Yet many of them were on remand in Holloway for several months.

(f) Work

Work is another activity which prison may provide for prisoners. Prison Rule 1[1] states that 'the purpose of the training and treatment of convicted prisoners shall be to encourage and assist them to lead a good and useful life'. Work in prison might therefore constitute an opportunity to carry out that purpose and convicted prisoners are required to work. Unconvicted remand prisoners cannot be required to do so as they are, theoretically at least, presumed innocent. However, while remand prisoners arguably do not experience a need to work, few of the research sample women had job skills or work experience and training in prison might have increased their job prospects on release.

The workshops at Holloway, capable of employing up to 90 women, were not operating during the research because of staffing problems.[3] Prison officers were supposed to be on duty in the workshop whenever it operated, but the staff were assigned first to essential tasks. The enormous drain on staff for court escort duty and the deliberately staff-intensive design of the new Holloway effectively closed the workshop, just as it affected other activities. On court days as many as 75 officers (out of a total basic grade staff of 279) might be away from Holloway on escort duty.[4]

The only work routinely available in Holloway in 1984 / 1985 was the work of keeping the prison going, work traditionally expected of female prisoners. A small core of women prisoners made up the Holloway workforce. When Pam was sentenced to imprisonment she became part of the kitchen workforce. She was an obvious choice, as a first offender sentenced for a cannabis charge. She got up at 6.30 a.m. to work from 7.00 a.m. until 5.30 p.m. on weekdays and until 1.00 p.m. on weekends. The pay was minimal.

> *'Last week I got £2.75. It goes up about 5p every week you're here. They knock 3p off for using the telly.'*

It speaks volumes about the regime in Holloway that Pam considered herself lucky to have her 'paid' job in the kitchens. The alternative would have been lock-up for a large part of the day. For that reason even the ancillary job of wing-cleaner was considered something of an advantage.

> *Chris had become wing-cleaner on her unit to escape lock-up. She scrubbed the communal areas not cleaned by the individual prisoners, responsible for their own cell cleaning.*
>
> *'I get let out to scrub the floors. I'm quite pleased. I get out at 8.00a.m. and I go back at 12.00.'*

Scrubbing was carried out in an archaic fashion. Devices such as sponge mops were not in evidence; instead the women got down on their knees and scrubbed. The floors always appeared very clean.

> *'You have to do things needlessly' remarked Celia, a woman on unconvicted remand, who had experience of hotel managing and catering. 'You scrub with scrubbing brushes. Do you think these floors need a scrubbing brush? That's to make you feel your place. We're only remands, but we do it too.'*

These old fashioned methods might be the result of management ineptitude or intent. When there is no other work for the prisoner population, the organisation may well try to make the existing work last as long as possible.

(g) Lock-up

Ultimately what affects conditions more than anything else is lock-up. Within Holloway the timetable varied between wings. The unit holding women immediately after entry as they awaited a more permanent wing had a highly restricted schedule:

> *'On D1 you can't work. There's nothing to do. You can't go to education. It's a 23 hour lock-up. You have to eat in your rooms. I haven't been out for exercise. They haven't got the officers to do it.'*

Clearly the wing for receptions presents particular administrative problems. Women have recently arrived. There is a good deal of paperwork under way. Decisions about where to place each woman are in train. Institutional concerns take precedence, particularly at the busy initial stages of a woman's introduction to prison, often as

49

an unconvicted remand. Close confinement for 23 hour periods is no way to experience the first impact of separation from home.

At the other end of the spectrum was the less restrictive timetable on the wing for pregnant women. Although more flexible than D1, the routine was characterised by monotony and inactivity. Anne, sharing a dormitory designed for four with five other pregnant women, described how a typical day was spent, waiting for meals as a chance to be unlocked: 'If there are enough officers we have supper out.' For the convenience of running the institution the last main meal of the day was at 4.00 p.m., about four hours after lunch, the other main meal of the day. Supper at 7.00 p.m. consisted of a drink and cake to keep the women going until breakfast at 8.00 p.m. the next morning.

On this wing the schedule was sufficiently flexible to allow two periods of association, before tea and after supper, if staffing levels permitted. In practice there were occasions during the research when even on this wing the women only left their rooms at mealtimes to fetch and return trays. 'Sometimes we have to eat and do everything in our rooms.'

TIMETABLE for 24 HOURS

Night Lock-up

8.00 a.m. Breakfast. Up before then to wash in the sink in shared dormitory or cell; clean rooms.

9.00 Lock-up.

[Perhaps call for exercise for half hour in total]

11.30 Lunch.

12.15 Lock-up. Staff have lunch.

[**2.00 - 3.30 p.m.** Unlocked if staff available]

4.00 Tea.

4.30 Lock-up.

[**7.00** Supper — unlocked if enough staff; association]

8.30 Lock-up for night.

The locked door was a norm of Holloway life. As women were isolated in their rooms, so the staff on a unit were isolated. From the locked cell a prisoner sees very little – a glimpse of the corridor from the small eye-level hatch in the door, if it is open, or a limited view of the grounds from the window. Staff in the wing office cannot see beyond the unit, sometimes not even all the unit; the view is a blank corridor with locked doors.

The lock-up regime at Holloway appeared to be the product of a complicated mix of factors, such as staff shortages, design faults, prevailing attitudes and external demands. The most frequently cited reason was staff shortages.

The design of Holloway involves long distances between locations in the establishment. The lack of clear sight lines along these distances affects perceptions of security. The prevailing notion in 1984-1985, that for security/control reasons all or most doors between each section of corridor should be locked, hampered staff mobility and made it necessary for prisoners to be accompanied everywhere.

The illogicality of this situation is apparent when one considers the subsequent treatment of women like Chris, initially remanded in Holloway, allocated to Styal, a closed prison, to serve her sentence and eventually transferred to East Sutton Park, an open prison. She was sent to Styal because she had a history of drug abuse. In place of the tedium of Holloway lock-up she had a range of activities. Living in one of the house units she was trusted to move between the buildings at Styal: 'You can't just walk about aimlessly. You have to be going somewhere. But at least you can go.'

According to the staff at Styal and East Sutton Park she was later transferred to the open prison because she had been bullied at Styal by other prisoners. She described the contrast in regime at the open establishment.

'At Holloway all they do is lock you in. Here the majority of them don't like the locking up system. They don't like having keys. I think they're happier. They even crack jokes. It makes you feel almost human.'

The conditions in Holloway had felt more like punishment to Chris than those at Styal and East Sutton Park. Yet she had been unsentenced at that point. Her offence was social security fraud involving a small amount of money; with several previous convictions behind her, she had never been convicted of any form of violence. Was her behaviour likely to be so different, in terms of security risk, at these different stages in her prison career, to warrant such different conditions?

The various aspects of conditions described had the effect of

51

punishing women remanded to Holloway. Punishment is not the legitimate aim of remand in custody, nor the stated aim of the prison system when dealing with remands, but it is the practical effect. One might question the justification for such forms of punishment for sentenced prisoners. For remand prisoners it is unacceptable.

Punitive conditions can arise in establishments like Holloway because there is no clear compelling mandate for more humane conditions upholding the civil liberties of prisoners on remand. Each of the areas of prison life discussed are covered by rules or regulations of differing status. Exercise, for example, is a statutory requirement under Prison Rule 27. There are Standing Orders, established by the Home Office and of ambiguous legal status, concerning hygiene, clothing, exercise, physical training, education, work and many other areas not dealt with here. The Circular Instructions, also issued by the Home Office and also of ambiguous legal status, though clear as directives to Governors, add another layer of guidelines.

This material is not organised in a coherent and easily usable form. The Prison Reform Trust has provided a lucid and practical guide to the Prison Rules,[5] but the Home Office's 1981 commitment to revise the Standing Orders has resulted in the publication of only four revised Standing Orders.[6] Copies or summaries of these rules and regulations were not readily available on a day to day basis to staff operating in Holloway; indeed they appeared to know little about them. Prisoners did not appear to know much about them either.

Thus daily life ran on the basis of unwritten operating rules, which appeared to take precedence over the written rules. In Kit's case, the 'rule' about not borrowing clothing took precedence over the legal entitlement to exercise, until Kit, with an officer's tacit agreement, disregarded the rules.

Such illogicalities arise in the prison system because there is no coherent body of legal minimum standards in England for conditions in prison. Although there is no instant solution for the appalling conditions in some English prisons, minimum standards are a necessary first step towards improvement. They would provide the missing point of reference for operating prisons and serve as a declaration of intention for those working and living there.

Without minimum standards there are no depths to which the conditions in prison may not sink. There is constant danger that the pressure to meet external demands takes priority over every other consideration, including the rights and human dignity of the people within the prison. Most vulnerable among these are the captive population, but prison conditions obviously affect prison staff, too. They make for difficult and degrading working conditions.

The lack of minimum standards leaves prisoners with no legal basis for complaint, however squalid their conditions. It also allows *ad hoc* rules to grow up and the exercise of broad discretion over the prisoners' lives. In these circumstances there will always be some individuals who will behave unjustly and abuse a system which is wide open to abuse. Minimum standards do not rule out such abuse, but they tend to limit its scope.

It is important that minimum standards should be developed with the remand population specifically in mind. The conditions in which the presumed innocent and unsentenced are held are, paradoxically, usually the worst conditions to be found anywhere in the prison system.

There is, however, another unrecorded story. At any given moment in recent times as many as a hundred women on remand may be held in police cells. There the conditions of hygiene and clothing are worse than in Holloway; exercise, physical training, education and work are virtually non-existent and lock-up constant.

It is important not to forget this lost population locked out of Holloway because since 1983 the actual remand population has consistently exceeded the population ceiling negotiated between management and staff at Holloway. At that time, as during the research, the situation was even less tenable than it is today, because there were actually empty units in Holloway standing unoccupied. As of November 1987 Holloway is officially certified to have normal accommodation for 479 women under 'Fresh Start', the new Prison Department management initiative, and there are no unoccupied units.

Since 1985, when this research was concluded, lock up has been reduced, so that cell doors may be open during the day time for some ten hours, roughly between 7.30 a.m. and 7.30 p.m., excluding lock-up for staff breaks and lunch. This improvement is highly commendable and has occurred without any major physical changes to the fabric of Holloway. It is important that the ground gained should be safeguarded. Whilst the law is an unwieldy means of creating change, it can be a useful instrument for protection against reverses. Legally enforceable standards focusing on individuals in prison, whether staff or prisoners, are the logical practical next step towards maintaining better conditions.

Legislation is, however, notoriously slow to materialise and implementation still slower. There are a number of practical remedies which would help women on remand immediately.

Holloway must improve the use of its facilities. The way that hygiene and clothing is organised should take account of the

53

remand population. It should not be supposed that because women prisoners are permitted to wear their own clothes they necessarily have an abundant supply of adequate clothing. One of the great common denominators among the Holloway remand population is their poverty. Adequate supplies of clothing should be made available for women on remand who are in need, and particularly to allow a change of clean clothes or adequate clothes washing and drying facilities before court appearance. Bathing and clean clothing should be linked so that if access to baths/showers is limited, at least clean clothes and especially clean underwear are available after bathing.

The organisation must also note women's additional hygiene needs relating to menstruation. This incontrovertible biological need has at times been downplayed by prison management. Adequate supplies and additional access to lavatories and showers should be available at all times when needed. Access to the facilities already existing in Holloway should be organised so as to take account of the hygiene implications of using the same basin for washing bodies, clothes and eating utensils.

Existing requirements for exercise and other legal entitlements which form the core of prison activity should be prominently posted to remind prisoners and staff of this priority. Education for remands should be geared to the immediate practical needs of that group, even if this means an orientation more towards social welfare rather than academic work.

Work is not an activity of prime relevance to the remand population, but not all training in employable skills requires periods longer than are spent on remand by many women awaiting trial. To the extent that this activity can be encompassed during the months spent on remand in Holloway it is surely common sense to offer it instead of inactivity.

Provision of activities within the prison regime ultimately depends upon maintaining staff numbers at the levels agreed as appropriate for the establishment. The long standing problem of acute shortage in middle management of senior and principal officers[7] indicates that the career structure for women prison officers needs re-examination.

Unlocking should be institutionalised as the norm for operations, so that it becomes difficult, and ideally impossible, to slide back to the days of continuous lock up. Ultimately this depends upon maintaining agreed staffing levels, steadfast reinforcement of management ethos and priorities and systematic training before work and on the job in dynamic security – keeping order without frequent locking up through enhanced staff team work with prisoners in small units.

Information

Prison is a confusing place. There is a clear need for information both about prison life in general and about particular events as they relate to the individual. An obvious starting point is the moment of entry, the reception process through which arriving women pass, many of them unfamiliar with the prison system or with Holloway.

Many remands are thrust unexpectedly into custody and arrive at Holloway, if they are lucky enough not to be locked out, late in the day, tired and bewildered. When women first arrive they are often still confused about where they are in relation to their homes, what actually happened in court and how long they are likely to be in custody. They do not know what to expect of the criminal justice system or in the prison and nobody tells them, except in terms of orders to be carried out immediately:

> *'Put your things down over there.'*

> *'Go into that room and put on this dressing gown.'*

They may not understand that this is leading up to a bath, a medical examination or even a strip search, until they are being told to step inside a partly screened area of the office:

> *'Drop your dressing gown. Lift up your arms. Turn right around. O.K. All done. Put it on again.'*

At Holloway the observed reception routine included a perfunctory strip search during which the staff and prisoners appeared equally anxious to complete the procedure as quickly as possible with a minimum display of emotion. There was so little warning before strip search that the researcher found herself observing the first of a long series without the prisoner's consent. Nobody else thought about asking any of the women, remanded or sentenced, whether they objected to being seen nude by an additional observer. The strip searches were observed by any of the officers and nurses who happened to be in the room at the time. Most of those not actually charged with this function were seen to look away quickly.

There was no introduction to explain what was about to happen. Unless they have been through it before, the women found out as it happened.

There was also no clear explanation of procedures for dealing with pressing problems. The research indicated that the most urgent matters on the minds of women entering Holloway on remand related not surprisingly to the people or homes they had left behind. These problems and how they are handled form the subject of separate discussion later in this chapter. The point to note here is that the reception procedure focuses on what **the system** needs in order to process the arriving prisoner. There is no regular mechanism for dealing with urgent outside problems at this stage nor for reassuring women with problems that there will be an opportunity eventually to handle emergencies.

As will emerge later, quick solutions to urgent needs depend upon the goodwill and energy of individual reception staff and are entirely at their discretion. Since help comes, if at all, in this haphazard way, the efforts of staff go unnoticed and unrewarded, although in the prisoners' eyes these first acts of assistance and humanity may be the most important. Equally there is no routine mechanism for feedback to prisoners to let them know that the problem has been resolved or that a message has in fact reached someone on the outside who can handle it.

The lack of information which characterises remand women's entry in prison affects their ability to exercise their rights and causes hardship. The difficulties of availing oneself of due process whilst in prison have been discussed in Chapter Two. The confusion and tension experienced by women entering Holloway on remand through inadequate orientation and information compounds their difficulties in dealing with their cases. What might appear superficially as an administrative failure has serious civil liberties implications. The reception process can be a kind of punishment in itself.

Lack of information may occur by default rather design. Either way it is an unacceptable fact of life in Holloway from the moment of entry. The situation is not entirely rectified as women spend time in Holloway. Prisoners' dependence on information from other prisoners tended to reinforce preconceptions about the prison system and to polarise attitudes.

In closed environments information and access to the channels of communication hold the key to power to an even greater extent than is true generally of life outside the prison system. When the organisation fails to recognise this salient fact, information may be used in ways which run counter to the stated objectives of the institution.

On Tuesday it was learned that Gloria was scheduled to be transferred to another prison on Thursday. She was due to have a visit on Thursday from a relative travelling over a hundred miles to see her. She was anxiously awaiting the visit. The wing officer informed the researcher of the transfer but said: 'Don't tell her. We don't tell them until the evening before they go.' Gloria was not able to let her visitor know of the change of plans and she arrived on Thursday to find that Gloria had gone.

When asked about this decision the wing officer explained that this delay of information was in the best interests of prisoners. Sometimes transfers had to be cancelled and staff did not want to raise false expectations. Another officer joining the discussion pointed out that it was they who would bear the brunt of a prisoner's disappointment, even though they had no hand in the decision.

Gwen was awaiting allocation to serve her six month sentence. She had arranged at court for her mother to bring her child to see her in Holloway before she was moved out of London. It was decided that Gwen would go to East Sutton Park in two days time, because the Holloway population was at its ceiling. If Gwen had been informed of this plan as soon as it was made, she might have managed to notify her mother, who was not on the telephone. She was informed on the afternoon before her departure and in interview appeared in acute distress at the prospect of being virtually out of reach of her mother and child.

In Gwen's case the officer in question expressed her strong wish to retain the information about Gwen's transfer. It appeared to be an example of use of information to enhance a sense of control; she felt that it was within her discretion to choose when to inform Gwen. In the course of the research there were several instances of women prisoners reacting strongly and at times with adverse consequences to themselves (e.g. three days prospective loss of remission) when they suddenly heard at a late date of an impending move. The strength of their reaction appeared to be linked to the shock of an important change in their lives about to occur without prior warning.

It is perhaps inevitable in an establishment operating by crisis management that sudden events overtake prisoners. What is less acceptable is that there should be a standard practice to create such crises artificially. One may hypothesise, on the one hand, that in a life over which staff feel they have little control, it is important to create means of control. If this is the case, the result is counterproductive, in the sense that it fuels hostility between prisoners and staff, increasing the stress of prison officers' work. The end result is too often a polarisation of positions which benefits no one.

Alternatively, or perhaps additionally, one might hypothesise that this kind of situation arises from mismanagement. Those working in Holloway were aware of being judged not by positive achievement, but by conspicuous problems or failures.[8] The atmosphere of crisis management underlined the belief that only mistakes were noticed. Trouble sparked off attention, but daily productive work might well go unnoticed. Running any large organisation in this way leads people to adopt habits to minimise taking risks and maximise anonymity. Whether information is withheld by intent or incompetence at whatever level within the organisation, the upshot is deprivation for prisoners and erosion of staff inmate relationships.

Theoretically the need to provide prisoners with general information is recognised and catered for by the information booklet prepared by the Prison Department. In practice copies are not always available at Reception, or even next day at the Reception Board.

The material was written in a style that assumed literacy and familiarity with English. Those are assumptions which are not justified by the experience within the establishment or by this research. The education department dealt regularly with cases of functional illiteracy or minimal reading skills among the Holloway population.

The internal population profiles indicated that among the considerable group of women in Holloway for drug offences (ranging from 28% to 20% of the population in successive surveys during 1984 and 1985) a majority was non-British. African women made up the largest group, commonly involved with drug importation charges.

The research found that while some African-born women were articulate in English, others could barely understand it and were virtually unable to communicate in it on all but the most mundane matters. At Reception Board, interviews with totally non-English speaking prisoners were observed to proceed by sign language, and in one case with the aid of one officer's tourist Spanish.

Even for those who had no literacy or language problems, the available information was regarded as of marginal use.

> 'They pass out these little green books. Nothing tells you what Probation are there for – what they actually do.' The booklet did describe some basic entitlements of unconvicted and convicted remands. However, it was not focused on the practicalities of life in Holloway in a way which would be easy for newcomers to grasp.

It is axiomatic that good management involves telling people what to expect. At Reception there was an obvious need for several kinds of information in a variety of forms. Since the research period, the education department has helped to translate the prison's written material into other languages.

If the traditional method of written information is used, the pack produced by the Prison Reform Trust illustrates how this can be achieved in plain English, which is easily understandable and addresses practical issues. The pack is produced and distributed entirely independently of the prison service.

Women entering Holloway need orientation. There is plenty of time for it. Women in the samples waited long periods at Reception before they were moved out to the prison wings. The process does not have to be staff-intensive. It might be achieved by a repeated message on a tape or video. There would be some initial cost for producing the message; video and tape equipment was available in Holloway at the time of the research.

The benefits would be several. There would be the immediate effect of letting women know where they were, what would be happening that day in the Reception process, the next morning at Reception Board and on the following days. It would explain how to proceed to deal with urgent problems. All this would take some of the pressure off Reception staff who have to deal with the mass of paperwork attached to new entry.

The orientation process would also help to allay in part the palpable tension at Reception, by reducing the stress of unfamiliar surroundings and occupying the attention of arrivals who otherwise wait in Reception with no clear idea of what they are waiting for. In addition certain potential problems for the prisoner and the prison might be identified at the outset, such as reading and language difficulties. When a non-English speaker arrives in Holloway it should be possible to identify her mother tongue so that if, among the varied staff in Holloway, there is someone who can speak that language, she is available at Reception Board or at some point during the following day to communicate basic information to the prisoner. At Reception Board it would be useful to post a list of personnel with language skills, for reference in difficult cases. Without this use of the human resources hidden among the Holloway working population some foreign nationals will continue to be severely disadvantaged.

In addition to these practical and somewhat mechanical remedies there is a need to rethink the ways in which information is used in Holloway. English prisons are more secret places than their counterparts in many other countries. The application of the Official Secrets Act to everything that happens in prisons has led to a preoccupation with secrecy far beyond all rational justification on security grounds. The automatic reaction appears to be not to inform. This state of affairs is likely to persist until the law is changed, despite some signs of greater openness by the Prison Department in allowing outside research. The situation is unhealthy when the overall policy of secrecy invites misuse of information at a variety of levels as an instrument of control and punishment.

The remedy must lie at least in part in a change of emphasis by management and staff at all levels, away from fear of communicating and manipulation of information. Communication skills should receive greater priority in the training programme for those who work in prisons to enable them to cope better with the hostility which is an inevitable part of prison life and also to avoid adding to it by unnecessarily repressive practices.

Relationships in Prison

Women remanded in Holloway do not suddenly cease to need personal relationships. They are frequently isolated by dislocation from those with whom they used to relate. As a consequence of life on remand they suffer many forms of affective deprivation. This section examines how the possibilities for positive relationships among prisoners and between prisoners and staff may be undermined:

(a) by a network of largely unwritten institutional rules and discretionary practices;

(b) by displacement of emotion and distrust

(c) by defensive apathy; and

(d) by the predominant transience of the remand population and lack of continuity among the staff.

a) working rules

In theory the prison system has given up the policy of isolating prisoners entirely in walls of silence, although the underlying notion of contamination still has some currency. Instead of this general strategy to prohibit all prisoner contact there is an elaborate set of working rules, mostly unwritten and often confusing, which reduce personal contact. Frequently the expressed reason for these rules is administrative convenience, but prisoners ascribe other motives to those who operate the rules.

The working rules have some clear characteristics: they often concern petty matters and their rigid application gives rise to illogicalities.

> *Caroline was told that she could not trim her fringe 'because it would change my appearance and that was not allowed. But my appearance has changed because my fringe has grown. Where's the sense in it.'*

The rule against a prisoner changing her appearance presumably relates to the security risk if a prisoner is not readily identifiable. In this case the prisoner grew more unlike her original appearance on arrival as a result of unthinking application of the rule. In any event it could be argued that no one considered her a serious escape risk, as she was a petty offender, originally remanded in custody and subsequently serving a short sentence for non-violent offences.

Earlier in this chapter Kit's dilemma illustrated how the basic entitlements of prison life, such as a minimum of daily exercise, might be forfeited because of lesser regulations: she could not go out to exercise without boots, but she was not allowed her boots because they had stiletto heels; the only way to obtain boots for exercise was to break the rules against borrowing. There is an Alice through the Looking Glass quality about the more trivial conundra of life in Holloway.

There are rules not only against borrowing but also against gifts. This may be intended to eliminate potential conflict or manipulation, but it has the effect of cutting off the normal human intercourse that is particularly necessary for women separated from family and friends.

> *Jenny had been asking for a ball-point pen since the previous day in order to write her reception letter. Eventually she borrowed one from another woman prisoner, although she felt worried that there would be trouble if they were found out.*
>
> *Chris was given some shampoo by a fellow prisoner:*
> *'It's degrading to sneak around.'*
> *At Reception Board one unconvicted woman asked if she could have the lager which her friends had brought for her. 'It's still at the Gate. My friend in here got hers. They said it's too strong, but she got it.'*
> *A lengthy discussion ensued between the Assistant Governor (AG) and prison officer on duty (PO).*
> *AG: 'I can't see that Standing Orders have anything about strength. They're allowed half a bottle of wine or beer, so how did this rule about strength come about?'*
> *PO: 'They can't have strong stuff like barley wine or export lager.'*
> *AG to women prisoner:*
> *'I can't give you an answer now because I quite simply don't know, but I'll find out.'*

Later that morning, when a prisoner made a request to have beer brought in, the Assistant Governor stated: 'You can't have export, only ordinary lager.' Perhaps this is how practical rules are born? The matter is minor; there is no basic right to beer, although at the time of the research, under Prison Rule 21, an unconvicted prisoner might 'be supplied with food at his own expense, or that of his friends', a privilege abolished in March 1988. This case illustrates how a sense of injustice and frustration are quick to arise in the closed atmosphere of Holloway.

Out of mundane occurrences such as these grow bitterness and hostility. Staff may become tense and defensive about recurring allegations of unfairness levelled at individual officers. Staff often referred to 'the rules' in support of their actions, while prisoners frequently read malice into their behaviour.

In organisations which run on unwritten rules and considerable discretion there will inevitably be different interpretations of the rules giving rise to a sense of grievance among those on the receiving end. A recurring theme at Holloway was the way in which some officers allowed certain minor concessions whereas others did not. This variation sometimes appeared to coincide with length of service, as older, more experienced staff displayed confidence in setting their own boundaries, while the many young and inexperienced staff members tended to fall back for safety on 'the rules'. In practice they referred more often to rules learnt on the job from colleagues than to written guidelines.

(b) displaced emotion and distrust

In the absence of clear rules and guidelines it is not surprising that in daily prison life there is confusion and insecurity about what should occur. Inevitably the conflict between those held in custody and those instrumental in holding them there intensifies on a personal level. 'Lacking the means to complain about their conditions, prisoners become preoccupied with the behaviour towards them of Prison Officers.'[9]

It is to be expected that tension will exist in a place of involuntary confinement. The profound sources of stress – deprivation of liberty and dislocation from home – find expression through displacement of emotion on to the trivia of daily relations: 'why am I here?' is transposed to 'why can't I have my drawing paper, my hairslide, my belt, a cross on a chain?'

Distrust is a by-product further undermining relations in prison.

> *Melinda was worried about who would be looking after her child. However, when asked at Reception Board if she had any domestic problems, she shook her head.*
> *The AG persisted: 'Who has your daughter?'*
> *Melinda lied about the arrangements, as was revealed later in the research interview. She explained that she was afraid that 'they' would put her child in care. She had heard that if a mother has been in prison it is hard to re-assert her claim to look after a child once taken into care.*

For that reason she did not apply to see the probation department at Holloway. 'They'll put her in care and I'll never get her back.'

Conceivably the probation department might have been a source of support and advice in this situation, but after one talk with the department Melinda was determined not to talk about the situation at home. She, like others in the sample, viewed the prison probation department as part of the prison system. This may or may not be a misconception. Certainly the department might have felt obliged to consider interests other than solely those of the prisoner, if the child's circumstances had been reported accurately.

To the prisoner it is not clear where the probation officer's primary allegiance lies. This may not be merely the result of exaggerated feelings of isolation or vulnerability. The professional terminology developed by probation was noticeably absent in the prison: the woman prisoner was not the 'client'.

(c) defensive apathy

An alternative to hostility between prisoners and staff is apathy. Self imposed withdrawal from affective contact was observable among both groups of women. There was a switching off reaction to the cumulative stress of conditions and regime, a defence mechanism not uncommon in other stress situations.

Pam decided not to apply for an inter-prison visit with her co-habitee. 'I don't know if I want one now. I think I'd crack up if I saw him. I've got used to not seeing him. I don't want to upset myself.'

Melinda was initially forthcoming in interview about her anxieties for her child, which she had feared to express to the prison staff or to probation. Four days later the circumstances had not altered, but she was repeating doggedly that the baby was all right and that everything would be fine. She appeared unwilling to discuss the arrangements. Her dull repetition was in marked contrast to her previous energy.

Chris explained her code of survival. 'The officer on this wing comes up and says "That telly's filthy."' So I says 'I'd better get a cloth then, Miss. But I'd only just wiped it. You just have to get on with it and tune out.'

The same strategy may work for the staff, too. In one corridor resounding with shouts and bangs from a distraught woman prisoner, an officer sighed and said: 'After a while you learn not to hear it. If you didn't, you'd be mad too.'

One afternoon the researcher en route to an interview was admitted to a stairwell and found herself imprisoned. The bottom entry to the stairwell had been locked, but the door from the stairwell to the unit was also locked. The researcher knocked on the door to the unit. Voices of staff could be heard in the wing office, but nobody came. The researcher banged more loudly. Anxiety began to take over.

She banged and shouted; nobody came. After twenty five minutes an officer came to investigate and unlocked the door.

A woman in the remand sample said: "If you keep banging and make a big enough fuss, you'll get some attention." That was borne out by first hand experience. After the first few weeks of research in Holloway the bangings had receded into the background of the researcher's awareness, rather as a camera, focused on the foreground, consigns unwanted objects to a general blur. This protective move made an otherwise intolerable situation more tolerable.

(d) transience and lack of continuity

A major contributor to affective deprivation in Holloway was lack of continuity. Transience is an unavoidable feature of the remand prisoner population, but the lack of staff continuity at Holloway was not inevitable. Besides the rapid staff turnover peculiar to Holloway, staff appeared to be constantly on the move. Staff shortages were cited as the reason for the norm of last-minute assignments.

Whatever the reason, the effect was to fragment life within the prison and raise tension. Part of a secure and stable work environment is a certain predictability and continuity of arrangements. This was conspicuously absent from staff arrangements at Holloway. The eleventh hour assignments produced stress rather than novelty. An element of variety in staff allocation is important to alleviate tedium in any organisation. However, the injection of variety works best when planned and when seen to be planned. The *ad hoc* scheduling at Holloway underscored the sense of crisis management. This was the key note of work in Holloway.

Officers did not know which colleagues they would be with or on which wing they would be working from day to day. This diminished the opportunity for good working relationships with other staff, not to mention with prisoners. Professionalism in a prison context is predicated on the notion of some continuity of individual contact.

Melinda came through Reception Board as a sentenced prisoner and learned there that, contrary to her expectation on remand, she would not be allowed to have her baby with her during her sentence. She was clearly distraught at the news. Later that day she was escorted to exercise by an officer from the Reception Wing. She forgot her belt on exercise and asked the officer to locate it for her. Still later that day she was transferred to another wing to await allocation. She asked the officer there about her belt and the officer denied all knowledge of it. Melinda confused the identity of the two officers who 'looked alike in the uniform'. She insisted on having her belt back. 'It was only a cheap one, but my brother gave it to me.'

(Melinda and her brother had been adopted by different families when their parents were killed in a car crash). Melinda grew angry and abusive. She was placed on report and later told that she would not be assigned to the Holloway workforce, as the AG at Reception Board had indicated. This would have kept her close to her baby in London. She was transferred to Bullwood Hall.

In the organisation's terms Melinda had overstepped the mark of tolerable behaviour. Might her outburst have been avoided? She seemed to have difficulty distinguishing one officer from another. This may have been due in part to stress. However, the uniform, the absence of name-badges, and the use of 'Miss', so reminiscent of school, rather than individual names, all contribute to the anonymity of the prison staff. Add to this the shunting of staff and prisoners from pillar to post and one has all the ingredients for alienation. In management terms it is a counterproductive way of handling people.

The effect on prisoners and staff is arguably equally negative. Young staff find themselves moved around without that sustained contact with individual senior officers which is vital to proper on the job training. A study of officers working in Holloway in 1984 indicated high rates of stress and most widespread support for 'more continuity of staffing on unit' and 'adequate notification of changed duties'.[10]

The sheer physical strain of court journeys may be offset for staff by the opportunity to escape from the tensions of Holloway, but for the prisoners they are compounded by another set of tensions, about the court outcome, the presence or absence of a friend or relative and the chance to convey urgent messages or receive long awaited possessions.

There were signs that when some continuity did occur there was scope for the development of positive relationships between staff and prisoners. The small core of women prisoners making up the Holloway workforce knew individual staff by name. This group was one of the few constants in Holloway life. Reliance and trust had to be placed in selected prisoners for the establishment to function.

Another pocket of continuity was to be found at Reception. The officers tended to work in the same small team for at least a week at a time, with the same senior officer in charge. When the team worked well together, it mitigated the impersonal atmosphere of the Reception rush.

Kay stood tensely awaiting her turn in the Reception chain. When she came to fingerprinting she said 'You can't do that one. My husband cut it off.' There was a moment's silence in the Reception Office. Then the fingerprinting officer said 'I'll lend you mine, love, then , shall I?' Kay began telling the officer about the fight with her husband when she lost her finger and they moved out of the central office together, the officer carrying one of Kay's paper bags of miscellaneous possessions.

The benefits of greater continuity were observed when women in the remand samples were later tracked as sentenced prisoners at Styal or East Sutton Park. Although Styal is a closed prison for sentenced prisoners only, the staff appeared less visibly as guards. The dynamic at Styal was different, not least because there were many tasks to be done which involved sustained co-operation of prisoners with staff.

At East Sutton Park, an open prison, there was, as might be expected, a more relaxed atmosphere. To a striking degree control was by personal contact. Staff pointed out that there was no 'lock up' cell in which to confine problem prisoners. 'If it's there, someone will want to use it and put someone in. Putting someone in doesn't solve anything. It just puts it off.'

The confidence underlying this attitude was in sharp contrast to the anxiety and defensiveness at Holloway in 1984-85. More recently at Holloway the contrast appears to be less dramatic. A move towards greater continuity of staff working in small teams has contributed to a different perspective on the control problem. The concept of dynamic security has gained ground in the United States: it means the maintenance of a safe prison through the relationships between staff and prisoners organised in small units and involved together in activities throughout the day; during the day the norm is unlocking.

There are practical remedies for the poor relationships which can arise in prison, particularly with a changing and numerous remand population. The working rules about relationships between prisoners require careful rethinking; especially where unconvicted remand prisoners are involved basic assumptions need to be questioned. In an entirely separate unconvicted remand population it would be neither relevant nor appropriate to guard against the supposed potential for contamination by experienced offenders by minimising personal contact. A practical improvement at Holloway since the research has been a more systematic attempt to concentrate the unconvicted remand prisoners on separate wings.

There are unspoken fears and undercurrents in a large female establishment about important issues deserving attention. A whole series of questions concerning single or mixed gender prison populations require consideration. Lesbianism among the women staff or prisoners is a subject often skirted around but never thoroughly addressed in the prison context. Yet it merits consideration by prison management to identify what part it plays in the dynamic of relationships between prisoners and between staff and prisoners. Until the question is aired internally it will be difficult to construct a realistic set of working rules concerning personal contacts within the prison.

The working rules about personal contacts need to be rethought and clearly stated. Staff and prisoners should know where they stand in these matters, to the extent that personal relationships can be the subject of regulation. Ideally this exercise would establish certain basic guidelines and remove a good many trivial rules which have no basis in logic, common sense or humanity.

Continuity of staff should be a priority whenever possible, with the norm of team work in small units to enhance the possibility of positive relations among colleagues and between staff and prisoners. Training of staff before and on the job must emphasise the distinction between remand prisoners and sentenced prisoners. The balance between guarding and caring for remands needs reconsideration in the light of the rights and entitlements of unconvicted persons.

Links with the Outside

Remand in custody is by definition a disruption of a woman's normal life. The effects of going to prison on personal lives on the outside vary with the circumstances of the individual, but certain common threads ran through the sample cases which point to serious systematic deprivation. Many cases involved urgent practical needs as well as longer term problems. Primarily these centred around economic distress and family difficulties.

(a) coping with crises

The distress of dislocation struck acutely for some women at the moment of separation from home. Some had hoped for a successful bail application and had not seriously expected to be remanded in custody when they went to court that day. Suddenly they found themselves unable to go back home and make arrangements. If someone they knew was at court they might be able to rely on that person to sort things out, at least temporarily after a snatched word or two. Often the women had no link with probation or social workers at court. Many times it appeared to be the police who stepped in to fill the breach, taking instructions about the child to be fetched, the oven to be switched off, the cat to be let out.

Often worries about these simple practical matters remained unsolved and occupied remanded women on the long journeys to Holloway. The long wait at Reception exacerbated their anxiety as they sat and dwelt on the problems. Did the police let the cat out? There was apparently no mechanism for letting the prisoner know that all was well. For her the crisis remained unsolved.

There were also anxious people on the outside, wondering what was going on. There is no easy system for obtaining information or passing messages to prisoners.

> *One evening late at Reception a relative telephoned five times trying to locate a woman remanded in custody. She had not come to Holloway. This much Reception was able to establish. After much searching through papers the senior Reception officer found a note of the police central clearing number. The caller rang back to ask Holloway to check again, because the police were unable to say where the woman was. Eventually it was confirmed that the woman had been locked out of Holloway and was being held in police cell accommodation somewhere in London, the precise location to be ascertained the following day, when the police had collated the information about the previous night's intake.*

Lock out is a serious and recurring problem. There should be safeguards to ensure its permanent elimination and a functioning information system to help family, friends and legal representatives to do what they can for women caught up in this appalling situation.

It is essential that the urgent needs of the arriving remand population of women, at Holloway or in police cells, are recognised and that the system is organised to take account of them. They are no new and surprising phenomenon. Women remain the mainstays of most households, if not financially then certainly in other senses. It is to be expected that crises, even chaos, will ensue if they are suddenly removed from the home.

Yet, when many of the sample women arrived in Holloway at the end of a long court day, they faced a Reception process geared to the prison's administrative needs. The conscientious prison officer struggling with Reception paper may try to juggle the pressing problems of a stream of new arrivals, but at this moment of critical need the considerable social work dimension in the situation of remanded women should not depend on the goodwill and stamina of busy Reception officers.

There was no Probation presence at Reception beyond the 'nine to five' schedule. Unfortunately, many receptions occurred after those hours. If Probation maintained a presence throughout Reception (i.e in the evening until 9.00 p.m. and at weekends) urgent needs might be identified earlier and action taken. The Probation input is not guaranteed even at Reception Board on the day following arrival. Probation has a statutory duty to see the non-adult prisoners. For the convenience of the probation department these young women were usually scheduled to be seen first on Reception Board. Probation officers saw some women while they were waiting for Reception Board, but many slipped through the net.

There is some debate as to whether it is the probation officer's role to handle practical social work problems. Certainly the probation officer has traditionally been the third party link in communications between the prisoner and the outside. Whoever is the appropriate person for the job, there is no doubt that the work is there to be done.

Coping with critical problems on the outside is not made easier by the lack of access to the telephone. If a probation officer or social worker were on shift to deal with urgent calls the pressure on the reception officers would be reduced. Prisoners might handle their own calls, with a probation officer or social worker monitoring for security purposes, if this seemed a risk.

There are sound practical arguments for the investment of time and human resources early in the process of entry into Holloway.

Urgent domestic problems do not disappear when they go unattended. They tend to be compounded. In the long run the probation department and social services may find themselves dealing with far more intractable problems if matters are allowed to deteriorate. In addition the lack of attention to these needs, which appeared to recur with striking regularity in the changing remand population, is a major source of tension within Holloway.

The absence of an adequate system for coping with crises at the outset, i.e. at Reception or Reception Board, seemed to be attributable only in part to resource problems. In part it arose from a lack of clear recognition of the problem's existence and of the prison system's obligation to remand prisoners not only to bring them back and forth to court, but at the very least not to contribute to the harm done to their home life and not to compound the difficulties of reintegration into the community. An enlightened prison system might be expected to assume the affirmative obligations to counteract the harmful effects of remand in custody by taking positive practical steps to alleviate problems on the outside.

(b) increasing hardship

Most of the women in the samples came into Holloway already experiencing economic difficulties. Their frustration on remand was increased by the knowledge that pressing economic problems awaited them on the outside and continued to deteriorate while they waited powerless inside. Several of them described feeling caught in a downward spiral of hardship.

A snapshot view of Holloway's unconvicted remand population on one day during the research confirmed these research indications. The vast majority (82%) were not in work. Those who had jobs were not highly paid and many had part-time or occasional employment.

The more detailed information for the smaller samples indicated that in addition to this poor work situation most of the women were living in accommodation which they did not own. They had in the main council rentals, not always in their own names. Most of the sample women were collecting support payments of various kinds, almost exclusively from public funds rather than from individuals. Thus, although the majority had children with whom they were living, and no constant adult male in the home, they were not receiving child support payments from fathers of the children. Several were receiving basic welfare support and heating allowance and some food support for the children in addition to child benefit. The majority reported being in financial difficulties characterised by debt or arrears in payment, such as council rent arrears.

The picture which emerges is of women coping marginally with a number of domestic and financial responsibilities. When they are taken into custody the precarious structure of their personal lives is immediately threatened.

Diane came out of Holloway and sent in her child benefit book, which was out of date by then. Four months later she was re-arrested and came back to Holloway. She had still not received a new book It had taken three weeks to sort out her social security claim 'and it's still not sorted out properly.' This family of a single mother and small child did not have money in the bank to tide them over the wait while the bureaucratic red tape was unravelled.

May was remanded in custody, but subsequently succeeded in her bail application on condition that she reside where her probation officer decided. She stayed in a hotel while her probation officer was looking for a hostel place for her; her former drug addiction made it difficult to find a hostel which would accept her. The hotel cost £16 per night. She was receiving £3 per day accommodation from Social Services. 'I had to bump it' in the hotel to find the money. She left to stay in a flat with friends, violating her bail conditions, and was returned to Holloway.

Women with some modest means found that remand in custody meant that they were likely to see their resources rapidly dwindling. Few had back-up from family or friends able or willing to assist.

> *Celia was facing a long wait for trial in the Crown Court. She was trying to arrange for her possessions, including some furniture, to be stored now that she would have to give up her rented flat. She asked bitterly how she could manage this from inside Holloway.*

> *Sophia had to keep up her hire purchase payments while she was on unconvicted remand and she had only a small amount of savings, which she feared would be exhausted before her case came to trial. Her rent was already in arrears and she did not have enough money to cover the rent and the hire purchase repayments.*

Council rentals may be paid by the local council for women in prison for up to nine months, if the relevant application is made. By a quirk of bureaucratic logic, heating allowance is no longer payable, regardless of the fact that the family of a woman remanded in custody may still need a warm home. Even if eligibility for benefit were less complicated, it presupposes that the woman understands how to arrange for it. However, it appeared from the samples that women on remand tended to be ill-informed about their entitlements and practical advice was hard to come by. Even if they do understand what it required, the considerable paperwork involved may not be sorted out from inside Holloway, given the distance from home, the delay in prison mail, the lack of telephone access and the general confusion which characterises remand in custody.

In the end women not infrequently leave Holloway with significant rent arrears; one woman in the sample had lost property, including clothing, when her landlord seized them in lieu of rent. Several women were homeless upon their release, two having been evicted. Others faced imminent threat of eviction and still others had lost their places on the housing list.

These situations recur too frequently to be treated as exceptional. Many of the women remanded in custody start off close to or below the poverty level. Remand in custody traps them more completely in the cycle of deprivation. Practical intervention is necessary to reverse this trend. In establishments like Holloway a more regular and dynamic social work support service is essential. There may be various candidates for this role and no reason why it may not be shared, so long as somebody takes final responsibility for ensuring consistent follow-through of advice and assistance.

Since 1984 NACRO's Women Prisoners' Resource Centre has

demonstrated that concrete support can be organised with the co-operation of those working inside Holloway and other women's prisons. The project assists women in the Greater London area with housing problems, including protection of tenancy, work, and training.

The work of the project highlights the need for liaison between Holloway and local councils and DHSS offices. Because of the degree of dislocation experienced by women on remand liaison is complicated and recent changes in the social security regulations have reportedly not made the task easier.[11] Much time in custody is wasted which could be used to work through these problems. Ideally a social work/welfare unit might operate from within Holloway, drawing upon prison staff, probation and other experts working in contact with statutory and voluntary agencies in women prisoners' home areas.

A senior staff officer commented: ' We could handle the welfare work. Probation doesn't want to. It might need more people, but often it might just take a phone call.'

(c) family troubles

Women on remand suffer, as most prisoners do, from the very fact of being away from home. Some of the women in the samples had families abroad; almost always they were women allegedly involved in drug offences, usually illegal importation as couriers.

> *Ellen had not heard from her family at all. It had been two months since she sent the first letter to Bombay. Could she telephone? The Assistant Governor on Reception Board informed her that Probation could arrange to make a telephone call on her behalf in an emergency, but there was no probation officer at Reception Board. Ellen had to make an application to see Probation. 'I did that last time, but I never saw anyone.' 'Yes, well we'll do it again' replied the AG on a note of resignation.*

For other women the lack of contact with their families was a source of anxiety because the arrangements for the care of children might be precarious. Whereas at one time in the case history of every woman in the sample, that woman had assumed the primary responsibility for her child(ren)'s care, this was no longer true of the women repeatedly in prison. Their children were with relatives (mostly the maternal grandmother) or in care.

For women less far advanced down this road, relatives and friends assumed the care of children in *ad hoc* arrangements which might shift over the course of the woman's absence. This dependence on the goodwill and financial aid of others over an indefinite period was fraught with tension.

Visiting presented an additional strain on these arrangements. The cost of travelling to and from Holloway might be considerable for families far away. When the household depended on benefits, as was often the case, the expense might prove prohibitive. The family of sentenced prisoners may apply for financial assistance to cover the expenses of prison visits. The system works by reimbursement of expenses incurred. This does not solve the problems of a family hard up for cash, with no firm guarantee of reimbursement even if they could borrow the money.

Financial constraints were not the only obstacle to visits. The visiting entitlements of the unconvicted remand prisoner are in practice not always available to women remand prisoners. It is ironical that it should be the 'female' system that carries this basic flaw. Male remands in local prisons are often closer to their families. Female prisoners, who are more often the affective centre of the household and assume the primary duty of care for children, are subjected to greater deprivation.

There are a number of practical ways in which the present situation might be improved: cash grants for planned visits and special visiting facilities at Holloway to take account of the likely involvement of small children would alleviate some of the burden, and a more flexible approach to cumulative visiting time for those coming long distances.

Easing of communications with the outside, especially when family and child carers are concerned, would make a difference and again the most obvious change would be direct access to telephones and removal of censorship of prison letters to speed up written contact. The old arguments of security risk seem to fall away when one considers that a prisoner may talk with a visitor without being overheard, although within sight of a prison officer. Any information constituting a security risk might be passed on at a visit as easily, if not more easily, than by letter. Checking prisoners' mail is costly, time consuming and wasteful. Human resources might be far better used.

Ultimately improvements to the present state of female prisons will fail to alter the basic unfairness of their organisation: the sparse distribution of facilities for women will ensure that a harmful effect on their personal lives persists. The present system needs reorganisation to keep female remands local. If that entails mixed remand centres with separate gender units, the difficulties and risks must be better managed than in the past. Yet more than reorganisation of the prison system is required.

Do those deciding on bail or custody acknowledge the practical realities of their decisions indicated by this research? Do they weigh the potential harm to the public of releasing on bail women defendants, usually charged with non-violent offences, more realistically against the probable alternative: dislocating a woman from home and perhaps contributing to the disintegration of her personal life or of a family. The majority of women on remand eventually receives a non-custodial sentence. If the alleged offence is such that this outcome is likely, there seems to be no persuasive argument for remand in custody which can outweigh its potential harm.

This chapter has focused on how the realities of life on remand may affect the personal lives of women in custody. It has emphasised those aspects of Holloway which impinge on remands generally – the conditions of daily life, access to and use of information, the relationships within the prison and contacts with the outside world. The next chapter looks at special care, a function fundamental to the idea of the new Holloway. It describes and examines remand women with special needs – pregnant women and mothers with babies; drug dependent women; and women who are 'disturbed'.

Notes

1. The Women's Royal Voluntary Service operated once a week at Holloway supplying clothes donated for charity.

2. H.M. Chief Inspector of Prisons, *Report on H.M. Prison Holloway*, 1985, p. 24, s. 4.05.

3. Plans for the later redevelopment of Holloway included provision of 200 workshop places in new facilities.

4. H.M. Prison Service, *Holloway Project Committee Report*, July 1985, p. 10, s. 4.3.

5. J. Plotnikoff, *Prison Rules: A Working Guide*. Prison Reform Trust, 1986 and revised edition 1988.

6. None has been revised and published since 1985.

7. *Ibid.*, p. 2, s. 1.6.

8. The issue of positive feedback, as well as other aspects of the management of human resources, is discussed more fully in I. Dunbar, *A Sense of Direction*. Home Office, 1986, a report for the Prison Inspectorate and the Prison Department on which the writer collaborated.

9. Prison Officers' Association, *Prisoners' Rights – Real or Imagined*, 1986, para. 5. Although the point was originally made in relation to complaints procedures, it might equally apply to the relationships between prisoners and staff generally.

10. I. Posen, *Holloway Officer Stress Study*, 1984.

11. The effects of the new regulations have not yet become apparent, but it is likely that any changes will be felt most acutely by this population at the lower end of the poverty scale.

chapter four:
Special Care

This chapter is concerned with the special care of women remand prisoners in Holloway, the keynote for the new prison redesigned in the late sixties. Focusing on women prisoners' diverse needs for special care and the prison's response to them, the discussion challenges the assumption behind the replanning of Holloway; namely, that the future population of female criminal offenders would be sick rather than bad (in contrast to their male counterparts) and therefore in need of special care.[1]

The chapter traces the disparity between the plans and the present situation in Holloway in relation to three areas of special care:

- child care and pregnancy
- drug dependence
- care of the highly disturbed

Childcare and pregnancy

None of the women in the remand samples gave birth in custody, but the samples included two women with babies and a majority with young dependent children in the care of relatives or of the local authority.

> *As a remand prisoner Dee was forced to make what arrangements she could for the unpredictable period of her remand for trial at Crown Court. (In committal cases it was not unusual for the court administration to telephone Holloway with the trial date only the evening before the trial was due to begin). Her mother looked after the baby and another child while she was in custody. She eventually received a two year probation order.*

Prison department policy permits a woman prisoner to keep her baby with her in prison subject to certain conditions. Inevitably some discretion is exercised, although a number of criteria are established for screening potential cases. These centre on the child's age and the mother's history, especially any record of past violence against children or of emotional instability (including psychiatric history, attempted suicide or repeated governor's reports of violent behaviour inside prison). In addition, if the woman has not been caring for her own children prior to arrest, she may not qualify to keep her child in prison.

> *Briefly remanded in custody before she met her bail conditions, Melanie gave birth while on bail. Her child was just over a year old when she re-entered Holloway at the start of a one year sentence for deception. The baby was not allowed in prison with her, as she had hoped, because it would be eighteen months and two weeks old at her earliest release date; the cut off age for babies in the prison system is eighteen months.*
> *When she learnt suddenly at Reception Board that her baby would not be with her during her sentence, Melanie was distraught. Later the same day she was placed on report for abusing an officer and instead of being allocated to Holloway, where she would have been near her baby, she was allocated to Bullwood Hall, a closed prison, despite the fact that her offence was non-violent (deception).*

Not all those eligible to have their young children with them in prison thought that this was the best arrangement.[2] Those who favoured keeping their babies with them spoke of the problems of arranging for relatives or friends to look after their children for them or their anxiety that, in the absence of an adequate alternative, the children might be taken into care. Research indicates that this was no empty fear.[3]

On the other hand some women voiced anxiety about the effect on babies of the closed atmosphere of prison life. Whether the unnatural life of the prison or separation from the mother is the lesser of two evils for the baby is a difficult question and one which continues to exercise the Prison Department.[4]

There is no gainsaying that prison life is not natural. Mothers and babies lived in an essentially all-female environment, restricted for many hours to the limited space of the prison cell. Although the doors were open during part of the daytime, observers estimated that mothers and babies spent about 18 hours in their cells. Access to the outdoors was limited to 30 minutes daily, and this time included the laborious manoeuvring of prams down to the ground floor. The mother and baby unit has since moved to new quarters on the ground floor, providing accommodation for more women and babies. After the evening meal (at around 4.30 p.m.) mother and baby were locked in until the next morning.

Although the new quarters provide a somewhat brighter and more spacious environment, the floor space available for crawling is restricted and babies are not observed crawling about the floors to the extent normally expected. Infants are routinely confined in pushchairs or held in their mothers' arms whether in or out of the cells. Researchers have pointed to the artificiality and constraint of the current arrangements.[5]

Among the sentenced and remand populations in Holloway a small group of women require special care because they are pregnant.

Although the lack of fresh air and restrictions of custody were not desirable for pregnant women, generally their material conditions were reasonably good in Holloway compared with police custody.

> *At arrest Anna was five months pregnant. She was held overnight at the police station. Initially she was placed in a cell with another woman and given something to eat at 4.30 p.m. Later she was moved to a cell with three others, sleeping on mattresses on the ground.*
>
> *In Holloway Anna was assigned to a dormitory room with five other women prisoners. She had a top bunk because she was less pregnant than the women on the bottom bunks. The beds were bunked because of overcrowding; the dormitories were designed for four rather than six.*

Although physical conditions in Holloway were an improvement on the conditions in police cells, the atmosphere at times was unpleasant.

> *As one pregnant woman came through Reception Board, the researcher heard a prison officer's audible aside: 'Ugh! Fancy anyone having sex with that.'*

The reasons for the custodial remand of pregnant women may be complicated or confused. They may have little to do with risk to the public, but more to do with perceived danger to the women themselves.

> *Anna was remanded in custody on charges of false representation. A German national, aged nineteen, she had lied about her period of residence in this country when she had tried to marry her lover, a British subject. The registrar had refused to marry them, querying the information. Anna described him as fatherly and worried about her. She thought that his attitude was due to the fact that she was white and her lover was black.*
>
> *The court, noting that she was five months pregnant, remanded Anna in custody for reports, ordering her passport to be retained. After the medical report revealed a normal pregnancy and no other problems, she was given a conditional discharge and left planning to marry her lover in Germany.*

Anna, an articulate student, contended strongly that the authorities had tried to help her out of her situation, against her own judgement. Pregnancy, like poverty, may be viewed by the courts as a condition meriting protective custody. This is not a legitimate use of custodial remand, but the lack of adequate community services may explain, though not justify legally, some courts' responses to perceived vulnerability in female defendants.

The case of Maud illustrates poignantly the inadequacy of official responses to a complex set of needs, compounded by pregnancy.

Maud was twenty seven years old, with an IQ of 67. Sexually abused as a child by her mother's friend, she had left home at 15. At 16 she began to live with a man many years her senior, whom she stated she loved. When he tried to run their home as a brothel, she burnt it down.

Serving her five year sentence she was briefly transferred to a psychiatric hospital on the grounds of mental subnormality. Failing to respond to treatment she returned to Holloway to serve out her sentence.

Since her release she had been thrown out by her mother and had been living rough for some time. She had been in and out of Holloway on a number of petty charges. During the research she was in Holloway having pleaded guilty to punching an arresting officer after stealing a bottle of milk. At Reception she reported having had no menstrual period for over two months. She was unco-operative when the doctor tried to examine her. The file noted 'PREGNANT?'

Maud spent one month in Holloway awaiting reports, which reiterated her past history and prescribed no treatment. She was released at court with a sentence of one month already served.

Six weeks later she was back in Holloway for assaulting a police officer who had tried to remove her from the local infirmary where she had crept in to sleep. Pleading guilty and remanded for reports, her pregnancy test proved positive. The prison medical file noted 'it would be disastrous for the pregnancy to continue.' Maud left Holloway still denying that she was pregnant.

Four weeks later she was back in Holloway and now visibly pregnant. She showed no understanding of pregnancy or childbirth and asked at interview: 'How do babies come?'

When questioned about her baby she said: 'They're going to look after it for me, but I'm going to keep it.' The doctor wrote on her file that she had refused an abortion and that 'any child would be in immediate danger once born and should be taken into care by the local authority at birth.'

Maud left court with another one month sentence already served on remand. The Holloway reports showed that her mother was unwilling to have her at home, but Maud had told the court that she was going to her mother. She had said the same on the previous occasion when she

Maud's case raises a number of difficult and important issues. The history of her pregnancy is a series of questions not followed through and decisions not taken. At a stage in her custody when there was still time for an abortion she had apparently refused one. The research interviews with her suggested strongly that she did not understand that under no circumstances was she going to be allowed to keep her baby with her. The choice was abortion or removal of the baby at birth, because the baby was deemed to be at risk.

The grounds for this assessment were not indicated, although it was probably linked to her record, particularly the arson. If that assessment was right – and the process by which it was made did not include advice to Maud either by a legal or other representative – the alternatives were stark: abortion or adoption. In those circumstances there was a further important question to be asked: was Maud capable of making an informed and knowing choice between those alternatives? That question did not appear in the files, nor any note of a decision that she was capable, although the bald notation that Maud had refused an abortion assumed that she could decide for herself. If that assumption was justified, there was still a strong case for providing an independent adviser experienced in dealing with women like Maud to assist her in understanding her options.

Cases like Maud raise difficult questions: the rights of the mentally handicapped, the ability to choose and procedures for consent.[6] Such individuals may gravitate towards the prison system and important decisions concerning them must be acknowledged as problematic and considered carefully with the involvement of those qualified to help. It is inadvisable to adopt a blanket policy with regard to the ability of the mentally handicapped to make decisions for themselves. Cases must be treated on an individual basis. There should however be a standard policy regarding proper procedures in such cases to ensure professional assessment and assistance and to guarantee as informed a decision as is possible under the particular circumstances. Decisions cannot be allowed to happen by default, as in the case of Maud.

Reading between the lines of the reports it is hard not to conclude that, because Maud was in and out of Holloway during the crucial first months of her pregnancy, the decision process on all sides was less organised and less rational than might otherwise have been the case. It was also clouded by the attitude of some of the medical staff; one doctor described Maud as being 'her usual fatuous self'.

It was never clear who had the final responsibility for her case – the court, the prison medical service, Holloway management, DHSS, her local G.P. or Maud herself. Everyone, including Maud, said that she needed help. The fact that she left Holloway with only the vaguest plans for support on the outside was cause for further concern.

It is beyond the scope of this study to speculate on the effect of prison conditions on the babies.[7] If there were adverse effects, it would be difficult to compare them with the potentially harmful effects of separation from the mother, particularly if that separation necessitated local authority rather than extended family care.

The grounds of Holloway, though not extensive, include open areas, partly grassed. Access to the open air should be a priority for these groups, the English climate permitting. The present arrangements for early evening meal and lock up until morning may suit the convenience of the establishment, but place undue restrictions on prisoners. Staff do not handle the care of infants, which is left to the mothers, who take a course in child care and are taught how to prepare babies' food and do housework.

A large staff complement is not necessary to ensure security and control in a unit full of babies. The spectre of an escape or riot amid the bottles and nappies is scarcely realistic. The staffing implications of a longer period before final lock up need not be excessively burdensome.

There is a strong case for rethinking contact between mothers and babies in prison and their outside families. Instead of mainly bringing outside child family members to the prison, with the mechanical and emotional problems that involves, there could be an extended system of home visiting for mothers and babies. There might also be arrangements for babies in prison to be fetched for home visits with other family members, so as to minimise the inflexibility and lack of variety of growing up in prison.

In addition to home visits, the visits allowance and arrangements for children on the outside coming to see their mother and baby sibling should be treated as a separate matter from other prison visits, with accumulated visiting time and frequent contact according to family circumstances.

However, improving living conditions and outside contact does not go to the more fundamental issue: whether these people belong in prison at all. The dilemma is a focus of continued debate. 'It is generally agreed that where possible babies should not be separated from their mothers, and that separation from her baby will prejudice the mother's rehabilitation, but there is little doubt that prisons are not suitable places for children to grow up in.'[8] This is an issue for the Home Office and ultimately for Parliament.

At present the courts interpret what they see as the public

interest in relation to women defendants and offenders with babies. The legitimacy and rationality of remanding pregnant women in custody and sentencing mothers with babies to imprisonment must be questioned. When the nature of the alleged or admitted/proved offence is not violent or does not involve large scale drug trafficking, there is no basis for assuming a serious danger to the public in releasing a pregnant woman on bail. Protective custody is *illegal* in these circumstances. If the presumption in favour of bail is to be a practical reality, courts must be obliged to articulate clearly their reasons for deciding that pregnant defendants or offenders awaiting sentence pose so real and present a danger to the community as to outweigh the undesirability of holding them in custody.

The imperative to consider all possible alternatives to custody, particularly when the offence is non-violent, has special implications for courts sentencing mothers with babies, because it is a sentence on the child as well.

Drug dependence

Current opinion has come to challenge some of the assumptions behind the new Holloway – particularly the notion that female prisoners in the eighties would rarely be criminally bad, like their male counterparts, but almost exclusively sick and requiring medical/ psychological treatment. However, one assumption which proved correct was that there would be a group involved in alcohol and other drug abuse, although, ironically, in this area the size and variety of problems were grossly underestimated.

Excessive drinking played a part in the lives of several women in the sample, but since drunkenness is no longer in itself an imprisonable offence, the habitual drunkard figured among the Holloway population only when her dependence caused other behaviour bringing her into conflict with the law.[9] The dependence on other drugs tended to accompany or supplant alcohol abuse in most of the cases in which drugs were a problem.

Holloway increasingly handles drug offenders and drug users. One of its major functions is to act as an interim or long term holding centre for women involved in drug importation. At the time of the research between one in five and one in four women at any given time in Holloway were there for drug offences, and three quarters of these for importation.[10] Some women move on to other establishments to serve their sentences, while others remain at Holloway as part of the core of sentenced prisoners.

The most frequently imported drug was cannabis, since the African women, the largest contingent, were involved almost exclusively with this drug. Few were reported users. If sentenced they drew heavy terms of imprisonment, not unusually four years or more. Until recently most women offenders sentenced to imprisonment had sentences under one year(84%).[11] The imprisonment of drug couriers has had a profound effect on the prison system for women, increasing the numbers substantially.

The special language needs, the dietary restrictions and the profound dislocation, geographically and culturally, of many of the (alleged) drug couriers combined to create a formidable set of new problems for establishments. In 1985 Holloway had neither identified nor addressed the size and nature of these problems. Since then the prison system has begun to recognise that this is an enduring phenomenon.

The drug problem in Holloway is not the same as the population charged with or convicted of drug offences. Although there was limited overlap between the couriers/suppliers and the users, the official charge/offence labels masked a larger hidden population with drug dependence.[12] In the admittedly small samples a number of property offenders had a drug habit to support: there were the known users like Chris and Tess, registered addicts charged with deception or theft; and there were the hidden users like Petra, relatively new to the habit and charged with shop-lifting.

Some drug dependence was noted in the medical screening at Reception. However, the examination tended to be brief and relatively superficial, relying heavily on information from the women themselves. Obvious cases of advanced addiction were detected from general emaciation and arms scored with needle holes, but many drug users did not favour this conspicuous technique.

Sometimes a woman was noticeably 'high' while at other times withdrawal symptoms during police custody, such as Tess clearly suffered, signalled drug addiction. However, there were also women passing through Reception without detection, the degree of dependence playing a role. Maria withdrew from drugs without medication because she did not want her drug addiction to be officially recorded.

When dependence is known, the woman's file is flagged and the withdrawal process begins or continues under medical supervision. At Holloway the process was rapid. May, Tess, Chris and Sally were all weaned off heroin in three days, with decreasing doses of physeptone.

Tess had received physeptone while in custody at court on Saturday. When she arrived at Holloway that night she was given a further 10 mg. On Sunday she had 10 mg three times, on Monday twice and on Tuesday her last dose. It was Christmas night.

When interviewed a week later she had not been sleeping well. 'I get sweats at night and my legs ache.' As a registered addict she had been on a regular methadone prescription since 1977. She pointed out that it would take more than three days to adjust.

Ironically the 'three day chop' was the product of public concern over the high levels of medicine dispensed at Holloway. Female prison establishments ranked higher than most male establishments in the official per capita medicine figures. Even taking into account the greater use of medicine by women in the population generally, the figures for Holloway were striking.[13] Public concern over the adverse press coverage drew a policy response from the prison system, with a concerted effort to reduce the use of medication in Holloway, including drug substitution for addicts. Some of the more acute withdrawal problems were experienced by women dependent on benzodiazepines (such as librium, valium, mogadon and other 'tranquillisers'). The women saw the policy of reduced medication as a move in the wrong direction, when it meant harsher withdrawal for them.

This policy may have backfired in some instances. Although the official statistics on medication showed changes, the habits of some women did not. Several women referred to the availability of heroin inside Holloway. One stated that during a previous period in custody she had taken heroin regularly and 'went out with a habit again'. Similar accounts were sufficient in number and given without apparent bravado to indicate that heroin, cocaine and cannabis are to be found inside women's prisons. The Chief Inspector noted in 1984: 'in many establishments . . . staff claimed that the smuggling of drugs into prison and their illicit use was on the increase.'[14]

If it were possible to eliminate entirely the entry of drugs into prison, the establishment would be faced with a daunting problem: there was a large number of drug users in various stages of dependence among the prisoner population. The prospect of a significant subset of the population in the process of withdrawal, either with or without official support, is not to be taken lightly.

Ideas for the new Holloway drew upon theories about the differences between male and female criminality and expectations of a female prison population that would be both decreasing in size and composed of special cases. As part of the medical model for the new prison there was to be a psycho-therapeutic unit providing special care for alcoholics and drug addicts. However, the size of the problem was vastly underestimated.

In 1985 the drug therapy unit, designed to deal with a maximum of 18 women, was inadequate for the size and nature of the population with drug problems. It relied heavily on sustained group work geared to a long term population, whereas the remand population was transient and most of the sentenced women were rapidly allocated to other prisons. During the research the unit was dealing with six women, on average, almost entirely by group therapy, while other women not involved in the programme were housed on the same wing. The Holloway Project Committee recommended continuing therapeutic work on this limited basis until the sentenced population at Holloway increased.[15]

The drug phenomenon in Holloway is a cause for grave concern. The criminal justice system has failed signally to keep pace with its development.[16] There is urgent need for a coherent and thorough-going policy on drugs in the prison system. It is necessary to know much more accurately the size and nature of the affected population. Holloway, as the chief medical/therapeutic centre for women, must identify the various needs of its drug involved population: the couriers from abroad with their particularly acute problems of geographic and cultural dislocation; the users, registered and unofficial with their short term problems of withdrawal and longer term needs for counselling and referral to care in the community.

As an establishment dealing with a rapid turnover of large numbers of remanded women, many of them involved with drugs, Holloway needs to develop a more sophisticated early screening system, offering immediate advice and information, coupled with strong supportive counselling to counteract the familiar syndrome of denial.

The drug therapy unit may continue to play a role for women who stay long enough in Holloway to make therapy feasible. It should help to refer women to projects such as Oak Lodge in London, offering a structured residential programme to ex-offenders with a history of drug dependence. However, it is vital that Holloway's approach to the drug problem should also focus upon the remand population to provide short term urgent support in the form of drug education and referrals.

The risk of AIDS contamination in the drug-using population has added an additional dimension and a sense of urgency to the special care role of Holloway. A recent survey of women received into Holloway identified a group of 55 out of a total of 208 women as 'at risk', because of reported habits of injecting drugs or prostitution.[17] Routine provision of practical information, general medical and contraceptive advice, hygiene, sex and drug education literature, counselling and an organised approach to through-care and referral is needed if the prison system's response is to be more relevant to the current drug phenomenon.

Care of the 'disturbed'

One of the primary functions in the plan for a new Holloway was a special unit to deal with the 'highly disturbed'. From the start the intended population of C1 involved three distinct groups, overlapping in some cases, but designated for C1 for different reasons:

the mentally disturbed women unsuitable for normal location on the wings;

women whose behaviour was seriously disruptive, i.e. control problems; and

women whose charge/offence indicated a need for special supervision.

This already complex target population was further complicated by external pressures – in 1985 C1 operated mainly as an assessment centre for women remanded by the courts for medical reports. Like the rest of Holloway, it had taken on the character of a predominantly remand facility rather than a treatment centre. The remand women on C1, exhibiting variously all, some or none of the characteristics of the target population, added their own different needs and problems to the formidable array confronting the unit.

The label 'disturbed' was applied not only to women diagnosed as mentally ill, but also to women exhibiting milder forms of personality disorder, as well as to women whose behaviour was primarily problematic because it disturbed others. The confusion clouded the important question as to the appropriate fate of these different sets of women.

Most remand women sent to C1 for assessment were not diagnosed as mentally ill. A minority (about one in four) were given hospital orders. In 1984 seven women, five of them on remand, were transferred from Holloway to outside hospitals under the Mental Health Act 1983. In such cases there was often a good deal of agreement among staff that the woman did not belong in Holloway. If a woman appeared mentally ill to those used to dealing with the mentally ill, why was she not in a hospital from the outset?

> *Sophia was held on pretrial remand on C1 because of the nature of her offence and for psychiatric assessment. She had allegedly, and by her own admission in interview, severed the hand of her neighbour because she believed that the neighbour had tried to murder her by placing 'poisonous insects from a live chicken from Liverpool Street' in Sophia's bed.*
>
> *'I got a knife when I saw her. I wanted to slash her face but I got her*

hand.'

The court had instructed that no plea be entered until medical/ psychiatric reports had assessed her ability to plead. 'The magistrates asked the attendants to take me out because I was shouting. I was trying to tell them it was unfair because I was revenging [sic] on her because she had inflicted deadly poisonous insects on me.'

When Sophia arrived at Holloway she was transferred directly from Reception to C1, her file flagged as a violent offender. She could theoretically have been remanded directly to psychiatric hospital for reports, but there was reportedly some reluctance on the part of psychiatric hospitals to receive violent individuals. The argument went that they were not equipped to deal with that kind of control problem.

After four weeks on C1 Sophia's reports were ready and the court ordered her transfer to hospital under Section 37 of the Mental Health Act 1983. The order specified that she must be placed within a month. After a further week on C1 Sophia was transferred to hospital.

Nurses and prison officers agreed that Sophia should never have been in prison. However, one pointed out that she might only stay in hospital for two weeks. 'She can go out at any time unless she's a section 41' (i.e. releasable only with the Home Secretary's permission).[18]

It is of course easy to criticise *post facto* the apparently unnecessary custodial remands for the majority of women sent to C1. For the minority needing hospital placement, like Sophia, prison was patently inappropriate. It is clear that considerable work needs to be done to assist courts in using the Mental Health Act 1983 properly 'to enable appropriate mentally disturbed persons to be taken into the health system rather than the penal system.'[19] Once a remand in custody has been made the condition that unsentenced prisoners can only be transferred to hospital if in urgent need of treatment presents an obstacle which does not exist for sentenced prisoners.[20]

The courts did not need to use custody for the majority of women assessed and subsequently released on bail or on non-custodial sentences. This disparity between the original decision to remand in custody and the eventual determination of release into the community is so glaring as to require serious rethinking. If medical assessments are required for such women, they should be arranged outside prison.

Then there were the misfits on C1, that dumping ground within the larger dumping ground which was Holloway. Maud was a case in point. She had no positive diagnosis of mental illness. Her problem was one of mental subnormality.

Maud was kept on C1 during her medical remands, because her behaviour in Holloway was at times disruptive. On one occasion she

broke a sink and destroyed floor coverings while in an 'agitated' mood.
She was prescribed largactil to be administered intravenously if she
refused to take it orally. Through medication Maud's behaviour was
kept within the bounds acceptable to the institution. She spent her time
in child-like bewilderment amid the wails and bangings of women
prisoners on C1.

Maud's stay in Holloway was an exercise in futility. Previous
medical reports had indicated that she was mentally subnormal and
not susceptible to treatment.[21] Further assessment on C1 only
served to confirm this view. Arguably Maud needed a supportive
environment in order to function at her own level. Placing her on
C1 confined her to a closed environment with virtually no activity
and almost constant lock-up.

Maud's case illustrates how an individual may fall through the
gaps in the state's system of care. There is no doubt that Maud
needed special care. The account of her pregnancy[22] raises doubts
about whether she received adequate care while in Holloway and
whether Holloway was the right place for her to be.

Maud's case also illustrates the way in which Holloway is used as a
last resort for women who do not fit easily into society and for
whom there are inadequate alternatives in the community. Early in
Holloway's history as an all-female prison the first Inspector of
Women's Prisons, Mary Gordon, voiced her concern about the way
in which women with all kinds of different problems were jumbled
together in Holloway: the criminal, the feeble minded, the
drunken, the paranoid among others.[23] It is all too easy to
recognise women in the new Holloway from her picture at the
beginning of this century.

The conditions on C1 at the time of the research were not
conducive to improving the state of mind of women held there.

During her five weeks in C1 Sophia remained in her nightgown, with
a dressing gown when it was cold. She lived in a single cell with a bed,
lavatory, sink and cupboard – physical conditions in themselves
comparing favourably with some other prisons.

In the morning Sophia was allowed out of her cell for about half an
hour to be served breakfast. 'We eat it in the sitting room or in our own
rooms. After that we go for brushes and clean our rooms. Then we are
locked in until lunch, when we don't come out; they bring it to us. The
only time we are out in the day is if a doctor comes to see an individual.
We're not unlocked until the following morning.'

This degree of lock-up and inactivity was antithetical to the notion
of a special unit caring for disturbed prisoners. It exacerbated the
individual's problems by adding the effect of isolation to her

existing difficulties; it built no long term solution and enhanced the probability of the revolving-door syndrome, for women like Maud; and it powerfully demoralised those continuing to work in a regime which they recognised as futile. It was also extremely upsetting just to be there.

> *'I try to read, but I seem to have little or no concentration.' As Sophia spoke there was a recurring background noise of shouting and banging. Once a bell rang, pressed persistently, by one of the women on C1, for over an hour without pause. A member of staff went to see what was the matter, looking through the door hatch to speak to the prisoner, who shouted abuse. There was a strong smell of urine. A prison officer tried to talk the woman into a calmer state. After three minutes of verbal and visual contact through the eye level hatch, the officer shut the hatch. The woman was still shouting and banging against the door. The noise could be heard throughout the unit. It was a characteristic background element of C1.*

In Holloway one reaction to signs of distress was often to neutralise the sometimes alarming, but more frequently upsetting impact, by defining the woman as disturbed. Being in prison is a disturbing circumstance. It causes upheaval, both emotional and material. Only people who are thoroughly institutionalised over a long period are likely to appear less 'disturbed' by prison than by life outside. For that very reason institutionalisation is viewed as a disturbed state.

When the prison refers to 'disturbed' behaviour, is it referring to behaviour which predates living in prison or to a reaction to prison life? The prevalent view of the disturbed woman was of a weak person, adrift from society's safe anchors. As such she might be pitied or despised, approaches which, whether consciously or not, re-asserted the controlling role of others in a situation otherwise fraught with stress.

One paradoxical outcome of this profoundly confused thinking was the policy concerning the discipline of 'disturbed' women prisoners. The Chief Inspector of Prisons highlighted the inherent conflict in the notion that 'the normal adjudication procedures could be applied to abnormal prisoners who were actually manifesting their disorders in bizarre behaviour at the time'.[24] The official response to the Chief Inspector's concern was vague, referring to the improved management structure as providing a better framework for reviewing the prison's options for responding to behavioural problems.

The inspection of Holloway revealed that a majority of the adjudicated women from C1 had conditions including brain damage and mental impairment. The pressures and constraints of a prison environment resulted in women being handled as offenders rather than as patients. In the end the aspirations of treatment were subordinated to the traditions of control even in that part of Holloway earmarked for special care.

Whether women on C1 were eventually diagnosed as mentally ill or not, whether they were defined as treatable or not, whether they received hospital placement or not, and whether or not the term 'disturbed' best described them, there was no doubt that there were women in Holloway who needed special care of different kinds.

One need more prevalent in the female prison population than among male prisoners manifests itself in the phenomenon of self injury. In 1984 serious acts of self injury among women on C1 – including horrific cases of self mutilation such as a woman gauging out her eye and another attempting to cut off her breast – attracted extensive media coverage and public concern.[25] Whatever explanations medical theory may offer, this is one of the ultimate expressions of despair. 'In a closed situation, dependent on others for their every need, unable to do anything about problems of home and family, uncertain as to what is happening to them and theirs, inmates inevitably suffer from feelings of helplessness and frustration'.[26]

This description focuses on the difficult problems facing many women in Holloway and the way in which the institutional response or lack of response compounds their difficulties. This suggests that whatever the medical response may be to the symptoms, the prison has a role to play in responding to underlying needs.

Another need for special care arose from a commonly shared history as victims of violence. One in three of the women in the admittedly small samples reported being abused, almost always by men, and usually by men known to them. These reports were the more striking because they were unsolicited; questions about victimisation were not part of the original interview framework.[27]

> One woman had lost a finger during a fight with her husband. He had closed the door on her hand.

> Two women had been sexually abused as children by friends of the family.

> Two women had been the victim of incest.

> Three other women spoke of having been raped.

Most of the women who spoke of being victims of sexual violence as children also talked of serious assault. A recent survey of women entering Holloway found evidence of abuse on a larger scale.[28] It is to the credit of Holloway's Psychology Department that it has tried to identify such problems. These efforts need to be incorporated into a new approach to special care, focusing on the Holloway population as it is today.

Not all women needing special care were housed on C1. One of the most 'disturbed' women in the sample was on the medical wing.

Patricia, like Maud, had a string of previous theft and/or minor assault convictions and a long series of medical/psychiatric assessments. Unlike Maud, she was highly intelligent. She had been treated ut psychiatric hospitals periodically since 1978 when she began, after the birth of her daughter, to exhibit wild and peculiar behaviour in public. The DHSS placed the child in care in 1979. Patricia was diagnosed as suffering from 'a personality disorder with paranoid and obsessional features'.

Reports during subsequent visits to Holloway indicated variously that she needed 'socio-therapeutic' or psycho-therapeutic help. At one stage a consultant psychiatrist referred her compulsorily to a psychiatric hospital on presumptive evidence of a psychotic illness. She had refused to go voluntarily. At the hospital she experienced hallucinations and schizophrenia was suspected. She absconded and after attempts to bring her back she was formally discharged, as there were insufficient grounds to hold her.

In 1985 she was remanded to Holloway for reports for refusing to pay her taxi driver and threatening him with violence because 'he was a dangerous escaped prisoner and a spy'. The consultant stated that another compulsory admission to psychiatric hospital would be pointless: 'She would, under a section of the Mental Health Act, be a very difficult patient to manage and this would serve no useful purpose if she herself did not consent to voluntary treatment.'

Patricia's case shows the dilemma facing those who work in the present system. Here was a person who was extremely difficult to handle. At times her delusions rendered her totally irrational.

She said at interview 'If you think you are my mother, better look at yourself in the mirror'; and she periodically cried out in the middle of the interview 'Who's that black man there? Take him away. He's a dangerous escaped prisoner.' There was no one there.

There were periods of relative calm when Patricia talked disjointedly about herself. However, these did not last long and she would ask: 'What have they put up inside me? I want to know.' She asked this question thirteen times over a two hour period.

Patricia received a month's sentence already served on remand. The Holloway staff expected her back before long. Although she did not fit neatly into the legal definition of a treatable person, it was clear to those working with her at Holloway that something was very wrong. She kept returning to Holloway where she was repeatedly assigned to C1 or the medical wing (depending on bed availability) because her behaviour was disturbing and unpredictable. There she was not treated at all but suffered visibly, often in incoherent distress. The staff suffered around her, from pity and frustration. Some persisted in their attempts to communicate with her, while others withdrew into dispirited lassitude.

The confusion about who should be on C1 and how it should operate is most poignantly clear in the more tragic cases among its population. These have drawn dramatic criticism from the press and concerned scrutiny from a variety of organisations including the Prison Inspectorate and the Holloway Project Committee. The Chief Inspector referred to the 'all too obvious conflict of roles which existed between those in medical departments and those concerned with operational aspects of the running of the prison.'[29] In 1985 the Project Committee described C1 as 'totally unsuitable for its task' and recommended *inter alia* a fresh initiative reconciling the professional approaches of the nursing and officer staff.[30]

The conflict between the medical and the prison ethos was clearly visible on C1 at the time of the research. One of the temporary agency nurses brought in to make up the numbers for the nursing staff was an experienced psychiatric nurse. She stayed at Holloway for six weeks, then left stating that she would not accept another assignment there. 'It is impossible to nurse in this place.' She explained how in practice, if a 'patient' rang for assistance on C1, she was often restricted to communicating with her through the hatch, because there were not enough prison officers available to accompany her to the cell. 'How can you treat someone through a door?'

Like most other nurses in Holloway at the time she was a black woman. The considerable friction observed on C1 where nurses and officers worked alongside each other included an element of racial conflict. One officer, disparaging the work effort of the nurses, remarked 'What can you expect? We only get the dregs.' The banter between officers did not generally extend to the nurses. In part this may have been the inevitable outcome not only of cultural differences, but of status differences. The officers on C1 were largely untrained in the specialist functions of the unit.

There was also evidence of tension within each group, particularly between the nurses of West Indian family background (who were in the majority) and the nurses from Nigeria. However, when the doctors arrived the nurses closed ranks and the prison officers looked on. Some of them complained of the difficulties arising from their responsibilities for control and the medical priorities. One of the few areas of agreement between the medical and the non-medical staff was the conclusion that 'most of them [the prisoners] shouldn't be here.'

It appeared that in Holloway, and particularly on C1, some experts felt the need to assert their professionalism by falling back on it in a defensive posture. This might have been the product of the ambivalent status of medical professionals in the prison environment. In theory the doctor's obligation was, as it always is, to the patient's health, but in prison, cut off to a greater or lesser extent from medical practice on the outside, the patient/doctor or patient/nurse relationship was compromised by the overriding aim of the establishment to maintain security and control.

This is a fundamental conflict. Management style and ethos may ease or exacerbate it, but cannot fully eradicate it. As in all large organisations, identity with and adherence to the norms of a wider professional group become restricted under the pressure to conform to the norms of the organisation. Day to day working contact modified the behaviour of the medical staff until it differed markedly from that of their colleagues outside the prison system.

There is undoubtedly scope for special care in Holloway, for many women with a variety of needs, who are not 'disturbed', or only in so far as it is normal to be disturbed by prison. The victims of violence are one group which has been identified. The research indicated many women with personal needs in relation to their lives on the outside, who were upset by their inability to deal with problems from inside prison and who required practical assistance.

The process of screening 'receptions' to obtain current information on the special needs of the entering population would be the first step towards addressing the practical task of caring for women prisoners. Part of this process should be a re-orientation to focus more attention on the remand population, largely ignored in the plans for the new Holloway but now a major element of the prison's work.

There is a case to be made for an early screening process to divert a number of women to hospitals rather than prison. The most obviously mentally ill might be remanded *directly* to psychiatric facilities for assessment;[31] courts already have this option, although they tend to use it infrequently,[32] the overwhelming majority of hospital orders occurring after assessment in prison.

Qualified expert opinion is not normally available at court for these initial decisions, so that in the first instance the courts must decide without specialised advice. The options are to refer on for expert assessment either on bail, in hospital or in custody. Courts tend to choose the last of these options in most cases. It seems likely that when an individual exhibits to the lay eye of the courts severe symptoms of disturbance they will continue to regard bail as too great a risk, whether this assessment is justified by later events or not. Under these circumstances referral to hospital rather than prison has the relative advantage of a theoretically less punitive environment where access to professional expertise should be easy.

At the other end of the spectrum many women might be remanded on bail for out-patient assessment at hospitals. A compromise solution for women whom the police and courts were reluctant to release on bail might involve release to a half-way house-cum-assessment hostel, providing a more sheltered environment and greater supervision/assistance than release to home. Conceivably some hostels for remand women deemed by the courts to have mental problems might have medical staff attached or resident to assist in speedy professional assessment. The hostel units would require links with visiting psychiatrists. There is no compelling reason why such assessment visits should take place in prison rather than in such alternative environments.[33] The object is to limit the damaging and costly use of prison for such women unless there are overwhelming reasons, other than their psychological state, to justify such use.

The figures on the outcome of C1 assessments of remand women indicate that the majority could be handled in this way. Such a change might remove as many as half the C1 remand receptions which place heavy demands on the unit and the establishment as a whole. It would also remove one glaring source of inequity as unconvicted or unsentenced women find themselves confined in one of the most disturbing places in the prison system.

Notes

1. These assumptions led to the characterisation of the new Holloway as a secure hospital. Home Secretary replying to a Parliamentary Question, December 1968.

2. A 1982 survey of female prisoners with children found that of those eligible to keep their babies with them in prison, slightly over half did not wish to do so. Nooney, Eastwood and Ray, *A Census of Mothers in Penal Establishments*, 1984.

3. *Ibid.*. 60 out of 653 mothers in the survey (i.e. over 8%) had children previously living with them who were taken into care when the mothers were sentenced to imprisonment. Of these children (113 in total) 32 were under the age of 5.

4. The Home Office has commissioned a developmental study of babies in prison. Liza Catan, *The Development of Young Children in Prison Mother-Baby Units*, 1988.

5. *Ibid.*

6. These issues have been debated fiercely following public interest in recent cases involving compulsory sterilisation.
   In re T. [1988] 2 WLR 189; re B [1987] 2 WLR 1213.

7.   An early internal study noted that inmate mothers interacted much less with their babies than did outside mothers, there was less stimulus from other adults and prison babies were less responsive than babies on the outside. C. Sloan, *A Study of Mothers and Infants in Holloway Prison,* 1972.

8.   House of Commons Social Services Committee, *The Prison Medical Service.* Report 3, 1986.

9.   The importance of excessive drinking may be seen from the fact that in the late 19th Century a majority of the women committed to prison were involved in the offences of breach of the peace, drunkenness, using obscene language or causing a nuisance. Dobash, Dobash & Gutteridge, *The Imprisonment of Women,* 1986, p. 93.

10. J. Shine, *A Description of Drug Offenders in Holloway* Holloway Psychology Department, 1984.

11. *Ibid.*

12. A survey of receptions by the Holloway Psychology Department found that of 47 women identified as drug users, 24 were on non-drug charges, mostly property. I. Posen, *Reception Survey,* 1987.

13. The annual reports of the Prison Department catalogue the disproportionately high rates for various kinds of medicines in female establishments, with Holloway clearly in the lead. The statistics are of limited use since they list per capita dosages, without specifying the dosage amounts. Tables compiled from the annual reports for 1979 to 1981 showed the phenomenally high use of medication at Holloway, relative to other establishments, male or female, and in particular the predominant use of psychotropic drugs. Radical Alternatives to Prison, *The Use of Drugs in Prison,* 1982.

14. H.M. Chief Inspector of Prisons, *Annual Report* 1984.

15. H.M. Prison Service, *Holloway Project Committee Report,* July 1985, p. 31, s. 8.8. Set up in 1985 by Lord Elton, the then Minister of State at the Home Office, to look into various issues including Holloway's special care functions.

16. In 1977 there were 1,731 notified narcotic drug addicts; by 1983 there were 5,864. In 1977 only 160 women were given custodial sentences (suspended sentences included) for drug offences, as compared with 419 by 1983.

17. I. Posen, *Reception Survey,* Holloway Prison, 1987.

18. A restriction order under the Mental Health Act 1983, Section 41.

19. Mental Health Act 1983, Section 48. See also the discussion of this issue in the Holloway Project Committee Report, *op. cit.,* p. 14, s. 5.3.

20. Report of the Home Office & DHSS Interdepartmental Working Group on Mentally Disturbed Offenders in the Prison System in England and Wales, May 1987, Recommendation 1.

21. The concept of the treatable individual is most clearly articulated in the Mental Health Amendment Act 1983.

22. See above, in this chapter.

23. Mary Gordon, *Penal Discipline*. London: Routledge, 1922.

24. H.M. Chief Inspector of Prisons, *Report on H.M. Prison Holloway*, 1984, p. 21.

25. NACRO Briefing Paper, *The Future of Holloway: A Summary of the Special Project Committee Report*, 1985.

26. *Self-Mutilation at Holloway*, DPS Series II, 1974.

27. The open-ended interview format allowed these accounts to come out unprompted.

28. I. Posen, *Reception Survey*, 1987.

29. H.M. Chief Inspector of Prisons, *Report on H.M. Prison Holloway*, 1985, p. 19, s. 3.13.

30. Holloway Project Committee Report, *op. cit.*, p. 32, s. 8.11.

31. An internal report on disturbed women recommended that 'at least those women identified as being schizophrenic could be diverted out of the prison system at an earlier stage'. Stewart & Shine, *Disturbed Women in Holloway*, 1985, pp. 4-5.

32. The Crown Court or a magistrates' court 'may remand an accused person to a hospital specified by the court for a report on his mental condition.' Mental Health Act 1983, Part III, section 35, (1).

33. These suggestions are in line with the trend away from psychiatric hospital places towards greater use of community care. They challenge policy makers to think imaginatively about variations on the traditional bail hostel adumbrated in the recent Green Paper. Private Sector Involvement in the Remand System, *Cm. 434*, July 1988.

chapter five:

Conclusions: Implications of the Study for Changes in Policy and Practice

This chapter draws together the main problems highlighted by the research and discusses the implications for policy. Part I considers the case of Holloway and the lessons derived from the research. Part II offers suggestions for immediate practical remedies which could be implemented now; these are framed with Holloway in mind, but might apply with modification to other establishments dealing with female remands or remands generally.

Part III discusses the policy implications for the prison system as a whole. Part IV raises more general questions about the criminal justice system.

Part I: Holloway

This study was undertaken when Holloway Prison was in a state of crisis due to the upheaval caused by changing to new accommodation as the final parts of the modern Holloway came on line in late 1984. Underlying the crisis was the further problem of population pressure. Beyond these quantifiable signs of stress there was a noticeable atmosphere of tension and demoralisation among many of those living and working in Holloway.

The research set out to describe and examine not merely a particular time of crisis, but the enduring patterns of life at Holloway and the recurring symptoms of a more permanent set of deep-seated problems. Much has since improved at Holloway but much of what is described in the research remains. The last two years have shown that improvement is possible through individual goodwill, skill and effort. The guarantee of lasting progress must, however, involve systematic changes as well as continued individual contributions.

Design for Women
The irony of Holloway is that the focusing of attention specifically

on the *female* prison population has given rise to results which are now recognised to be a great mistake. The grand design for a new Holloway was seen to be inappropriate before much of the building programme was completed. Even if the population had not deviated so dramatically from expectations, it is questionable whether the architectural plan would have served the original objectives.

The purpose here is not to criticise the details of those planning errors, but to draw out some general lessons:

1. prison buildings have to last through shifts in population and policy and should be built with the capacity to respond to change; and

2. a workable building is more than the simple sum of its mechanical parts. Prison design should be rooted in practical information and operating experience.

Holloway is not a workable building. It is based on a set of ideas about women prisoners and what should happen to them in prison which bears little relation to current reality. The problems of the physical plant seem to be contagious and infect the way people operate and behave. Ideally the new Holloway should be demolished.

It would, however, be simplistic to blame Holloway's troubles solely on its building. An example is the controversy over C1, the unit for the highly disturbed. The recommendations of the Holloway Project Committee for 'a purpose-built unit' to replace C1 are not likely to solve the problem of special care. The whole of the new Holloway *was* 'purpose built' on the medical/therapeutic model. It is intentionally staff-intensive in design and the physical plant isolates people. However, ultimately the problem is not one of architecture. It is a problem of philosophy. If the women on C1 are disturbed they need care in an environment other than a prison.

Crisis Management

The physical plant of the new Holloway however affords a striking symbol of a deeper problem. Even in 1985 when the plant was new, there were obvious technical weaknesses: for example, rain came in along the main corridor. The Works Department ran on a breakdown basis: they waited for something to fail before working on it, rather than performing routine maintenance. By analogy the whole of Holloway appeared to run on a similar basis. It was driven primarily by the need to respond to *ad hoc* external demands – court escort, assessment for court reports and the allocation of sentenced women at high speed to keep beds available for the next influx.

Many prison establishments are crisis-driven. The external pressures are undeniably great, but if they become the rationalisation for perpetual crisis management, prison establishments inevitably deteriorate to human warehouses.

The Remand Functions

Among its various functions Holloway is *de facto* a remand centre, a factor not anticipated in its planning. This report has highlighted the problems arising when remand prisoners are subsumed in a prison establishment and system which fails to accord full recognition to remand status and to consider what it means to carry out the duty of care for remand prisoners.

At Holloway this would mean reorganising priorities to embrace not only the mechanical tasks of fulfilling court services, but also the facilitation of bail and legal representation, social/welfare work, information and education services, as well as the provision for the special needs of drug dependents, the 'disturbed', pregnant women and mothers with babies.

Lessons from Holloway

Suggested changes focusing on the immediate and particular needs of women on remand are outlined in the following section. Four fundamental points lie at the core of these proposed improvements.

1. Prison management has no say in a decision which affects it directly: the courts' decision to remand women in custody. It is common sense, however, for prison management to focus energy and attention on practical systematic initiatives to reduce its population, within the terms of the courts' decisions.

The research indicates that some women spent time unnecessarily on custodial remand, because of confusion or difficulties over bail arrangements. It is indefensible that mechanical problems should make the difference between liberty and custody. Facilitating bail arrangements would help to prevent the recurrence of overspill into police cells in substandard conditions at a cost of £200 per person per night. It is morally and economically unjustifiable not to pursue this initiative.

2. Prisons depend to a large extent on the co-operation of their prisoner populations in order to keep operating. Better relations between prisoners and those who work in prisons are vital to the smoother and more effective running of prison establishments.

There is an inevitable tension between the kept and the keepers. Security (i.e. safety from escape), though essential, does not have to be the raison d'etre of prison staff. There are sound reasons to balance control and care tasks by drawing the energies of all who have to live together in prison into activities focused on the practical needs and problems of the remand population.

3. Early screening is a prerequisite for effectively dealing with the needs of the remand population. Just as the system needs to know more about women as they enter, so women entering Holloway need to know more about the system. A simple orientation programme at entry could provide the necessary two-way flow of information. Reception and Reception Board are critical points: getting it right at Reception may save time, money and suffering.

4. Change does not necessarily entail vast additional expenditure. The options suggested in the following pages do not generally involve large capital outlay. Holloway has many modern material advantages. Its problems relate to people more often than plant. Therefore the focus in the suggestions for change is on human resources (although exceptions such as the introduction of telephone access would undoubtedly involve initial capital investment and operating costs).

Nor are the proposed modifications predicated on large scale additional staffing, a crucial factor accounting for most of the prison budget.[1] They involve a different approach to the use of the prison's human resources. This implies a shift in management ethos and a re-orientation of staff effort. Such changes may involve some additional expense in the initial stages, for retraining and establishing new methods, but these could be offset by potential savings in the longer term. For example, it would take time and effort to set up a bail unit in Holloway, but arguably existing human resources might be redeployed to achieve this. If, as intended, the unit facilitated bail in cases like those found in the research, the reduction in time spent in custody would mean considerable saving in prison and in human costs.

Part II: Practical Suggestions

The following practical suggestions are made primarily with Holloway in mind, but might apply with modifications to any establishment dealing with female remands and more generally to all remand facilities. They consist of changes which could be implemented within an individual establishment.

A. Case Related Facilities

As a major female remand centre, Holloway should provide certain critical services for its many women prisoners involved in on-going court cases. These should cover all major aspects of due process, primarily recognition of remand status, representation, bail /custody, court appearance and report preparation.

1. *a duty solicitor/legal advice centre within the prison providing*

   (a) routine screening of all receptions for representation needs and alerting all receptions to the availability of this service

   (b) routine and basic information about the court process in the form of a written or taped information service provided in the prison library to alleviate the more common misconceptions and much anxiety and confusion

   (c) more sophisticated back-up help through advisers available for on the spot consultation at regular times

2. *improved access to outside lawyers through*

   (a) direct telephone access (see C.3. below)

   (b) writing materials readily available at entry into prison and thereafter

   (c) streamlining the laborious procedure of applications for letters through assistant governors

3. *a bail unit inside the prison*

   (a) operating from the point of entry into prison with automatic screening early enough to identify those for whom action is necessary

   (b) facilitating arrangements for those on conditional bail and straight remands in custody

   (c) providing designated staff to cover the post at all times when women enter the prison and available at regular times thereafter

   (d) if probation to share/assume task, ensuring presence of a probation officer required either throughout Reception (not just 9.00 a.m. to 5.00 p.m.) or throughout Reception Board

   (e) providing liaison with hostels for women, with particular attention to exploring places for women with drug-related histories

4. *improved facilities for court appearances*

   adequate hygiene facilities made available at prison or in police cells prior to appearance and clean clothing provision, or assistance in preparing clothing for court appearance

5. *accelerated preparation of reports*
    (a) improved liaison between the prison and local probation departments
    (b) early contact with the remand prisoner within three days of remand to reduce the traditional three week period

6. *recognition of remand status by structural divisions*
    (a) routine daily organisation to reflect importance of remand status
    (b) separate parts of Reception Board for sentenced and remand prisoners, to underline distinction of status and to separate the allocation task from the induction of remand prisoners
    (c) separate units within an establishment for remands versus sentenced prisoners
    (d) different security levels according to status, with provision for a variety of security levels within remand group (see also B.5 below)
    (e) activities tailored to the remand population's short term and urgent needs, especially those relating to due process, addressed specifically in all aspects of the regime, including education and information.

B. Conditions in Prison
In the absence of a code of minimum standards, the following areas of provision form the core of what is required for basic prison conditions consistent with human dignity.

1. *hygiene*
    (a) hygiene and clothing organised to take account of the remand population entitlements and particular needs
    (b) stock of adequate clean and fitting clothing to supplement private clothes where necessary, not only provided on volunteer basis e.g. by WRVS
    (c) clean underwear available after bathing
    (d) adequate washing and drying facilities
2. *exercise*
    (a) existing requirements for exercise and other legal entitlements should be prominently posted to remind prisoners and staff of this priority
    (b) exercise and access to the open air should be guaranteed for full period daily as per Prison Rules

(c) adequate clothing should be provided at all times to ensure women can go outside as entitled

3. *education*

(a) early screening for immediate needs such as English language education and information, with relaxation of protracted assessment and enrolment

(b) ongoing provision of key short term courses geared to immediate practical needs with orientation less towards academic and more towards practical skills and information e.g. how to write/give orally an orderly account of a sequence of events

(c) how to frame a request for information, letters to solicitors, Social Services, local councils

(d) how to tackle a social security problem, whom to contact, which information to obtain and from where

(e) how to arrange for payment of council rent during remand

(f) how to expedite transfer of child benefits to a third party in charge of a child

(g) agreed procedures for education staff to fetch prisoners and to work with the minimal prison officer complement necessary for security

4. *work*

(a) training in employable skills for women awaiting trial at Crown Court, who will spend the longest periods on remand

5. *unlocking*

(a) unlocking should be institutionalised as the norm of operations for remand prisoners (barring exceptional circumstances) with emphasis on dynamic security – the maintenance of order by active use of time in prison and developing relationships between staff teams and small units of prisoners

C. Communications

Communications and the proper and effective use of information are the key to improving relations within prison and between prisoners and the outside world. Particular aspects of communications are repeated in other sections to underline their crucial role in ensuring that prisoners are aware of and able to avail themselves of the suggested services.

1. *orientation centre at Reception*

    (a) written information such as the Information Packs pro-
    duced by the Prison Reform Trust and the Women
    Prisoners' Resource Centre in plain English, easily under-
    standable and practical, translated into other languages by
    Education Department

    (b) repeated messages on a tape or video, with personal access
    by prisoners, letting women know

    – where they are and what the place is like

    – what will happen next and what is expected of them

    – what will happen later and what they can expect

    – what to do (whom to see) about urgent problems

2. *early screening system*

    (a) identifying potential problems at the outset, such as

    – reading and language difficulties

    – drug dependence (see I.1. below)

    – special histories – victimisation, abuse

    – home problems

    (b) providing a list of personnel with language skills in
    Holloway at Reception and Reception Board to ensure that
    there will be a member of staff to speak in the prisoner's
    own language available at Reception Board (or scheduled
    during that day to avoid staffing disruption)

3. *a functioning communications system to provide assistance in the
    following key areas*

    (a) emergency service at Reception

    – screening for urgent outside problems

    – telephone access and service to relay messages or to find
    someone outside to deal with problem

    – routine mechanism for feedback to prisoners to let them
    know that the problem has been resolved or that a message
    has got through

    (b) direct access to a telephone, with probation or prison
    officers monitoring for security purposes, if deemed a risk

– to facilitate contact with families and friends and especially to minimise problems of separation from children

– to expedite consultation with lawyers

– to handle welfare problems, such as communications with DHSS or local council over housing or benefits

(c) removal of censorship of prison letters to speed up written contact, except in case of demonstrably over-riding security need

4. *up to date technology for management information*

   (a) computer files rather than card index to co-ordinate information, including, fo example court information that the defendant requires interpreter

   (b) updating property lists for remand population coming and going to streamline Reception paperwork and reduce delays at Reception Board

D. Rules

In the absence of a coherent and comprehensive set of rules governing what happens in prison and safeguarding the rights of all those who live and work there, daily prison life operates according to *ad hoc* rules whose origins and legitimacy are questionable and which are often known only by word of mouth. Unless this situation is regularised, conflict and inequity are inevitable.

1. revision and reorganisation of Prison Rules
                                   Standing Orders
                                   Circular Instructions

   production of indexed summary to be posted in prison and available from the library

2. statement of working rules of daily prison life, written and available to staff and prisoners with emphasis on minimum use of punishment for minor infringements of rules

3. published plan to implement minimum standards for all aspects of prison to alert staff and prisoners to basic level of conditions below which reality of daily life should not fall

E. Interaction in Prison

Although mechanical improvements may enhance the prison environment, the quality of life in prison rests ultimately on the relationships among the people who live and work there. Effective and humane prison management consists in recognising the importance of the human resources in prison and according staff and prisoner relations due priority.

1. emphasis on building relationships:

    use of names and name-badges for staff

    staff continuity in teams and locations

    norm of team work in small units

2. staff training before and on the job must emphasise:

    distinction between remand and sentenced prisoners

    balance between guarding and caring

    rights and entitlements of unconvicted and unsentenced

3. regular consultation between various staff levels to exchange information on practice and policy, including feedback from all prison officer grades on changes

F. Visits

Facilities for contacts with the outside should recognise the fact that many women on remand have a continuing role as mainstays of most households. Poverty is another important characteristic of the remand population, necessitating practical and financial assistance if the visiting privileges of remand prisoners are to be a reality.

1. cash grants for planned visits

2. special visiting centre facilities at Holloway to take account of the likely involvement of small children would alleviate the stress of long journeys

3. more flexible approach to cumulative visiting time for those coming long distances

4. special allowance for extra direct access to telephones for communications with children and child carers (see C.3. above)

G. Welfare

The research illustrates the many mundane social work tasks associated with women on remand, many of whom are poor and may have to make temporary and *ad hoc* arrangements for their lives on the outside. No one consistently seems to be responsible for this work. The need for a coherent approach to the welfare of women on remand should be recognised and the tasks systematically assigned and integrated into the work of the prison.

1. social work/welfare work using a combination of probation department, prison officers, education department and others in Holloway

2. working as a team, but with final responsibility for individual prisoner's programme of help clearly designated

3. providing intervention to halt downward spiral of deprivation by giving practical advice and assistance with
    housing problems
    work and training
    benefits

4. liaison between Holloway and local councils, DH and DSS offices and non statutory agencies, such as NACRO's Women Prisoners' Resource Centre

H. Child Care and Pregnancy

The anomaly of custodial remand of mothers and babies necessitates the exercise of particular care to ensure that the deleterious effects of removal from home are minimised as far as possible in the prison context. The decision to accept babies as well as mothers places the prison under a special obligation to provide proper facilities:

1. extra access for babies with their mothers to the open air in Holloway grounds as a priority

2. increased mobility inside

3. relaxation of constraints, such as the rule against having a baby in bed, to encourage relationship with mother

4. greater adaptation of environment to children's needs, including brighter decor, pictures, floor space to crawl

5. greater opportunity for group interaction for children and mothers

6. special regime (geared to special needs of children and mothers and reflecting the low security problems) including later night lock up,if necessary at all; later evening meal

7. extended facilities for visits from relations, special allo-

wances and arrangements for other children to visit (see also F, above)

8. special allowance for mothers and babies to make regular home visits to maintain contact with children outside

9. special arrangements for babies to go out of prison on visits to minimise inflexibility and monotony of personal contact

I. Drug Dependence

Holloway has failed to keep pace with the prevalence and variety of drug problems among women remanded in custody. The research indicates the limited capacity of the drug/alcohol therapy unit in Holloway to deal with the increasing drug involvement of the prisoner population and emphasises the need for more sophisticated strategies for early identification of problems and systematic provision of information, support and referral.

1. *screening and medical support system at entry focused on varied drug problems*

   (a) the couriers from abroad with their particularly acute problems of geographic and cultural dislocation

   (b) the users, registered and unofficial, with their short term problems of withdrawal and longer term needs for counselling and referral to care in the community

2. *drug therapy unit for women who stay long enough in Holloway to make therapy feasible*

3. *short term urgent support geared to transient remand population*

   (a) information and education on
   drug addiction
   drug referral programmes
   hygiene
   contraception
   AIDS counselling

4. *organised approach to through-care referrals*

5. *flexible withdrawal programmes to correspond to different levels of dependence and different drug histories*

J. Care of the 'disturbed'

Whereas the report has argued that many remand prisoners on C1, the unit for disturbed women at Holloway, should not be in prison at all, it is incumbent upon the prison to make every effort to cater for the needs of this group and to provide as humane a system of special care as is possible within a prison.

1. screening of receptions to obtain current information on the special needs of the entering population, early diversion to hospitals for most obviously mentally ill by speedy arrangements for medical assessment and liaison with outside hospitals

2. control of disturbed women should be handled as a medical and not a prison matter: external medical opinion required to pronounce prisoner 'fit' before disciplinary procedures can be applied to disturbed prisoners

3. priority for removal of C1 unit to new building to be constructed at Holloway (proposed in 1985 but still at planning stage)

4. responsibility for running of C1 to rest with prison medical service, in consultation with Governor; areas of conflict to be resolved by ultimate reference to the Director of the Prison Medical Service and to external professional standards for good medical practice

5. full staff exclusively composed of qualified nursing officers and other medical staff

6. agreement that nursing staff may unlock and treat prisoners on C1 Unit without prison officers, provided there are two members of nursing staff present

7. provision of regime on C1 incorporating extended periods of activity outside cells, including skills training

8. training of non-medical staff coming into contact with unit concerning the special ethos of a unit for disturbed women based on a medical rather than prison model

9. standards for handling prisoner corresponding to prisoner's designation as C1 prisoner whether inside unit or elsewhere within prison

Part III: Policy Implications for the Prison System

The female prison 'system'

There are problems inherent in the existence of a 'separate', numerically inferior, female prison system. Female prisoners do not represent a sufficiently large population to have warranted a thorough appraisal of their characteristics and needs. Their system is the poor relation of the dominant male prison system.

The logic of that system creates anomalies when applied, along with its assumptions, to female prisons. The research has pointed to the significant effects of dislocation, an almost invariable factor of female custody and imprisonment, because the choice of establishments for women around the country is so limited. Here lies a paradox: the female remand population is punished by the conditions of female custody, notably by dislocation from home, although in this society it is still assumed that women will take the primary role in parenting and care of the home.

Minor improvements to the existing state of female prisons will not alter the basic unfairness of their organisation: the sparse distribution of facilities for women will ensure that harmful effects persist. The present system needs reorganisation to keep female remands local.

The Remand Distinction

By historical accident there is a single system to imprison people on remand and offenders sentenced to imprisonment.

Establishments like Holloway deal with these different populations simultaneously. The result is that certain fundamental principles of justice are obscured: the presumption of innocence, the entitlement to due process of law and the unlawfulness of remand for punishment.

Prison policy needs rethinking to take account of the variety of the prison population, particularly in terms of remand / sentenced status and what that should mean for the way the prison system handles people. Many of the prison system's basic assumptions do not fit the remand population.

The general debate about the aims of the prison system continues. Despite the general confusion, there is minimalist agreement: the prison system should aim to make people no worse when they leave prison than when they arrived. Given the practical realities of our prison conditions this, while minimal, is no easy objective to sustain.

By analogy the prison system must aim to make people on remand no worse off with respect to their ongoing cases than they were before they were placed in custody. The research indicates that in various important respects Holloway does not fulfil this aim.

A blurring of distinctions tends to follow from mixing prisoners of different status. The logical conclusion is that there should be a separate remand system.

Existing remand centres are few and tend therefore to lead to dislocation, but this is not an inherent characteristic of remand centres. Local prisons, which currently cater for many remand prisoners, entail less dislocation than remand centres such as Pucklechurch or Risley.

The need to separate remand and sentenced prisoners has been lucidly argued elsewhere[2] and the research confirms the view that the conditions of remand in custody constitute a form of punishment which is entirely inappropriate for an unconvicted or unsentenced population. Since it may not be economically viable to operate separate local remand units for women, another possibility[3] is mixed local remand centres with separate units for men and women. The practical options involve a real dilemma, centring on the issues of mixed populations versus dislocation.

Mixed local remand prisons could be a serious alternative if due attention were given to the safeguards necessary to counteract the risks. Unspoken fears and undercurrents surround the question of single or mixed-gender prisoner and prison staff populations. Many women prisoners have had extreme experiences of victimisation, often at the hands of men. It is hard to eliminate sexual harassment from mixed institutions. There are pressures in single gender environments, too. Lesbianism among the women prisoners or staff in establishments such as Holloway is a subject often skirted around rather than thoroughly addressed in the prison context.

Neither alternative is ideal; it is a question of choosing the lesser evil. In mixed establishments there is always the danger that the numerical inferiority of women prisoners will result in less access to facilities, as well as the erosion of hard-won privileges. Ideally in mixed establishments there should be adequate provision to allow those women who need a single-gender environment equal access to the positive elements of prison facilities.

Minimum Standards for Prison Conditions

Changes in the Holloway regime since 1985 indicate that practical improvement is possible without any major physical changes to the fabric of Holloway, legislation or any new regulations. However, long term change for the better can only be safeguarded by statutory minimum standards.

Punitive conditions can arise in establishments like Holloway because there is no clear, compelling mandate for more humane conditions upholding the civil liberties of prisoners on remand. There is no official code of minimum standards in this country for conditions in prison.[4]

Minimum standards are no instant solution for the appalling conditions in some English prisons, but they are a necessary first step towards improvement. They would provide the missing point of reference for operating prisons and serve as a declaration of intent for those working and living in prisons.

Without minimum standards there are no depths to which the conditions in prison may not sink. There is constant danger that the pressure to meet external demands takes priority over every other consideration, including the rights and human dignity of people within the prison. Most vulnerable among these are the captive population, but prison conditions obviously affect prison staff, too, by creating difficult and degrading working conditions.

The lack of minimum standards leaves prisoners with no effective basis for complaint, however squalid their conditions. In the absence of standards established by legislation or declared by the Prison Department, prisoners have no grounds for redress in the law courts or through internal complaints procedures. It is of course true that many in the system, like Maud, would not be able to avail themselves of the protection of standards, or not without considerable advice and assistance. Even for prisoners capable of making full use of the law, the route to change is unlikely to lead through the courts with the frequency noted in other countries, such as the United States.[5] However, the prospect of even infrequent complaints for breach of the Prison Department's own standards, or lawsuits for violation of standards established by Parliament, would prove an incentive for change. The very existence of declared minimum standards, based on legislative or other authority, would create a powerful moral imperative.

Under existing circumstances grievances are directed, by default, not against the system which breeds them, but against the individual who happens to be on the front line.[6] It also allows *ad hoc* rules to develop and the exercise of broad discretion over the lives of prisoners. In these circumstances there will always be some individuals who will behave unjustly and abuse a system which is wide open to abuse. Minimum standards do not rule out such abuse, but they can limit its scope.

Minimum standards should be developed with the remand population specifically in mind. The conditions in which the presumed innocent and the unsentenced are held are paradoxically usually among the worst conditions to be found anywhere in the prison system.

Coping with Special Care
The criminal justice system has failed signally to keep pace with the drug phenomenon. There is an urgent need for a coherent and thorough-going policy on drugs in the prison system. As a first step prison establishments need to gather systematically much more

accurate information on the size and nature of the affected population.

Given the estimated scale of the drug problems among the prison population, small discreet drug therapy units, like the one at Holloway, are arguably inappropriate. Dealing with the variety of drug-related problems must be integrated into the mainstream work in prisons.

Whilst the need for specialists remains, there is a need for all staff to develop expertise. Drug problems are not a small aberration susceptible of treatment by a handful of specialists. It is a task for the prison service as a whole. Local and central management must adopt an integrated approach to dealing with special care as part of staff teamwork.

There will always be some people in prisons who need special care, for drug-related problems or for disturbed behaviour. Indeed, some cases of disturbed behaviour will inevitably arise as a reaction to imprisonment. People should not, however, be sent to prison because they need special care. At present the prison system acts as a last resort for some of the more intractable cases passing through the criminal justice system. Holloway is one of the dumping grounds.

Information

There is a need to rethink the ways in which information is used in Holloway. English prisons are more secret places than their counterparts in many other countries. The application of the Official Secrets Act to everything that happens in prisons has led to a preoccupation with secrecy far beyond all rational justification on security grounds. The automatic reaction appears to be not to inform. This state of affairs is likely to persist until the law is changed, despite some signs of greater openness by the Prison Department in allowing outside research. The situation is unhealthy when the overall policy of secrecy invites misuse of information at a variety of levels as an instrument of control and punishment.

The remedy must lie at least in part in a change of emphasis by management and staff at all levels, away from fear of communicating rather than towards manipulation of information. Communication skills should receive greater priority in the training programme for those who work in prisons to enable them to cope better with the hostility which is an inevitable part of prison life.

Part IV: Beyond the Prison System

The research stresses the need to reconsider some of the basic assumptions of the criminal justice system. It challenges the logic of remanding females to prison if they are non-violent and not involved in offences involving large amounts of money (e.g. organised drug trafficking), when the only legal grounds for refusing bail are the likelihood that the defendant will not appear, will offend while on bail or will interfere with witnesses. The research cases reflect the official statistics, which show that most women on remand are not charged or convicted of the most serious, violent offences. Many have family ties which would make it unlikely that they could not appear in court without being picked up by the police. Refusal of bail appears to be used as a punishment in some cases, with serious consequences for the prison system, as the research shows, both in human and in civil libertarian terms.[7]

The research gives examples of the harm caused by female remand in custody, not only to prisoners' ability to handle their court cases and but also to their personal lives. In the context of a society which still assumes that the main childcare role falls on women, the decision as to bail or custody should be rooted in a practical assessment of which is the lesser evil for society: disruption of the home/family plus curtailment of access to due process of law or the risk of a relatively minor offence being committed or the risk of the defendant disappearing.

The majority of women on remand eventually receives a non-custodial sentence. If the alleged offence is such that this outcome is likely, there seems to be no persuasive argument for remand in custody.

These facts about the female remand population challenge the rationality of current bail decisions. The research provides examples: can remanding a pregnant woman in custody on a charge of giving false information be justified on any of the three legal grounds for denying bail? Was the risk to society so great, her absconding so likely (especially when her passport was withheld) or an attempt to interfere with witnesses at all probable? This is an extreme example of the absurdities of the system. There are other examples, less egregious, but more common, of outcomes of the bail/custody decision which cannot be justified in law or common sense.

It is easy to criticise decisions with hindsight. It is, however, necessary to approach important decisions with the foresight that comes from looking at the facts. The evidence is provided by the Home Office. It is time that that feedback was reflected in a more consistently-informed approach to bail decisions.

If the presumption in favour of bail is to be a practical reality, courts must be obliged to articulate their reasons for custody more clearly and precisely than the current formulae – 'further offences' or 'unlikely to appear'. They should be obliged to explain how a female defendant who has no previous serious, violent convictions and is not accused of a serious violent offence, poses so real and present a danger to the community as to outweigh the undesirability of holding her in custody.

The implications of the Nottingham Justices case[8] for the way in which bail/custody decisions are made have been re-examined in the debate on the Criminal Justice Bill. The Government has accepted that the presumption in favour of bail is not compatible with such limited access to the courts for bail applications.[9] It has also acknowledged the need for better-informed decisions, both by the Crown Prosecution Service, when considering whether or not to oppose bail, and by the courts.[10]

Policy and practice must also change with respect to numbers remanded in custody for reports. Ultimately the best hope of improvement lies in finding ways of preparing reports outside the prison system. More attention should be given to the provision of local hostel accommodation in cases where the home is judged unsuitable; out-patient assessment places at hospitals for medical report remands; and hostel places for those with histories of drug dependence.[11]

The provision of remand alternatives in the community raises the question of the appropriateness of electronic tagging as a substitute for custody. The Government has confined its recent consideration of electronic tagging to the discussion on community sentences.[12] Besides the objections to electronic monitoring as intrusive and antithetical to rehabilitation, there is a grave danger that this new measure would be used by courts as an additional restriction for defendants or offenders whom they would formerly have released on bail anyway.

There must be much clearer thinking about the justification for remands in custody for reports when individuals have previously been on unconvicted remand on bail. Does that same individual suddenly pose a much greater danger to the public or present a greater likelihood of absconding; are pre-conviction and post-conviction custody intended as forms of short penalty (arguably they have that effect); or does custodial remand for reports arise from administrative convenience, as the court gives priority to professional rather than due process needs? None of these are appropriate reasons for custodial remand.

The courts are not the primary focus of this study, but inevitably the research calls into question the results of the court process. It is impossible to conduct research on women remanded at Holloway without coming to the view, shared by many of the people interviewed who work there, that a substantial proportion of remand prisoners do not belong in custody.

Notes

1. In the 1986-87 period out of a total net operating cost of £618,224,000 prison manpower costs accounted for £512,906,000.

2. Lord Windlesham, 'Punishment and Prevention: The Inappropriate Prisoner' in *Criminal Law Review,* March 1988.

3. A suggestion which goes some way towards this alternative – female units attached to male prisons – was recently put forward by Baroness Seear and Elaine Player, *Women in the Penal System,* Howard League for Penal Reform, 1986, pp. 14- 15.

4. A first step in the direction of minimum standards for prisons in this country was made with the NACRO code, which draws on the admittedly vague European Standard Minimum Rules and more precise examples from the United States and Canada in order to present suggested standards for physical conditions. S. Casale, *Minimum Standards for Prison Establishments.* NACRO, 1984.

5. Litigation concerning prison conditions predated the adoption of minimum standards in the United States and provided an important impetus to their development. Many jurisdictions now have minimum standards for prisons and prison systems have been forced to change by court sanctions for non-compliance, including the closure of prisons in extreme cases.

6. The argument is clearly made by the Prison Officers' Association in its review of complaint procedures, *'Prisoners' Rights – Real or Imagined?'* 1986.

7. The issues raised in the research reflect previous indictments of the bail system. M. King, *Bail or Custody.* Cobden Trust, 1971.

8. *R. v. Nottingham Justices,* ex parte Davies [1980] 2 All E.R. 775.

9. See the discussion in Chapter 2, above.

10. The Green Paper 'Private Sector Involvement in the Remand System' (Cm 434, July, 1988) notes the positive indications from recent bail information experimental schemes. The experience from these projects has led probation services to extend the initiative (cf the planned co-operative efforts of the probation services in the London region to provide bail information services).

11. The Green Paper (see note 10 above) refers to an expansion programme to increase conventional bail hostel places. The Government is considering the introduction of hostels offering 'more secure conditions, such as 12 hour curfew and a more structured daytime programme' in the context of private hostel management. (p. 2, s. 5).

12. The Green Paper 'Punishment, Custody and the Community' poses questions about the usefulness of electronic monitoring and discusses a new sentence, the supervision and restriction order, which might include tracking offenders' whereabouts.
    Cm. 424, July 1988, s. 3.20 – 3.24 and s. 3.27.

Selected Bibliography

Adler, F. *Sisters in Crime*. New York: McGraw Hill, 1975.

American Correctional Association. *Standards for Adult Correctional Institutions*, 2nd ed., January 1981.

Arrowsmith, P. *Somewhere Like This*. London: Allen, 1970.

Atkins, S. & B. Hoggett. *Women and the Law*. Oxford: Basil Blackwell, 1986.

Austin,R. 'Liberation and Female Criminality in England and Wales' in *British Journal of Criminology*, Vol. 20, No. 1, 1981.

Baldwin, J. & A. Bottoms. *The Urban Criminal*. London: Tavistock Press, 1976.

Bedford, A. 'Women and Parole' in *British Journal of Criminology*, Vol. 14, April 1974.

Bottomley, A.K. *Decisions in the Penal Process*. Martin Robertson, 1973.

Bowker, L., ed. *Women, Crime and Criminal Justice*. New York: Lexington Books, 1978.

Brink, B. & C. Stone, 'Defendants who do not ask for Bail' in *Criminal Law Review*, March 1988.

Brodsky, A. ed. *The Female Offender*. London: Sage Publications, 1975.

Buckle, A. & D.P. Farrington. 'An Observational Study of Shoplifting' in *British Journal of Criminology*, Vol. 24, No. 1, 1984.

Carlen, P. *Women's Imprisonment*. London: Routledge & Kegan Paul, 1983.

Carlen, P., J. Hicks, J. O'Dwyer, Diana Christina & C. Tchaikovsky. *Criminal Women*. Cambridge: Polity Press, 1985.

Casale, S. *Minimum Standards for Prison Establishments*. NACRO, 1984.

Casale, S. & S. Hillsman. *The Enforcement of Fines as Criminal Sanctions*. New York: Vera Institute of Justice, 1986.

Catan, L. *The Development of Young Children in Prison Mother-Baby Units*. Home Office, 1988.

Chambers, G. & A. Millar. *Investigating Sexual Assault*. Scottish Office Social research Study. Edinburgh: HMSO, 1985.

Cloward, R. & L. Ohlin. *Delinquency and Opportunity*. London: Routledge and Kegan Paul, 1961.

Cowie, J., V. Cowie & E. Slater. *Delinquency in Girls*. London: Heinemann, 1968.

Criminal Justice Bill [Lords], Report Stage, 28 June 1988.

Cullen, J.E. *The Prediction and Treatment of Self Injury by Female Young Offenders*. DPS Report Series I, No. 17, 1981.

DeFleur, L.B. 'Biasing Influences on Drug Arrest Records: Implications for Deviance Research' in *American Sociology Review* 40, 1975.

Dell, S. 'Remands of Women Offenders for Medical Reports' in *Medicine, Science & the Law,* pp. 117-127, 1971.

Dell, S. *Silent in Court*. London: Bell, 1971.

Department of Education & Science. *Report by H.M. Inspectors on H.M. Prison Holloway,* 1985.

Dobash, R.P., R.E. Dobash & S. Gutteridge. *The Imprisonment of Women*. Oxford: Basil Blackwell, 1986.

Dominelli, L. *Women in Focus: Community Service Orders and Female Offenders*. Nuffield Foundation, 1984.

Dunbar, I. A Sense of Direction. *Prison Inspectorate and Prison Department,* 1986.

Eaton, M. *Justice for Women*. Open University Press, 1986.

Edwards, S. *Female Sexuality and the Law*. Oxford: Martin Robertson, 1981.

Edwards, S.M. *Women on Trial*. Manchester University Press, 1986.

Eysenck S. & H. Eysenck. 'The Personality of Female Offenders' in *British Journal of Psychiatry,* pp. 693-99, 1973.

Farrington, D. & A. Morris. 'Sex, Sentencing and Reconviction' in *British Journal of Criminology,* Vol. 23, No. 3, 1983.

Faulkner, D. 'The Redevelopment of Holloway Prison' in *Howard Journal,* 1971.

Feinman, C. *Women in the Criminal Justice System*. New York: Praeger, 1980.

Giallombardo, R. *Society of Women*. New York: Wiley, 1966.

Gibbs, C. 'The Effect of the Imprisonment of Women upon their Children' in *British Journal of Criminology,* Vol. 11, April 1971.

Gold, M. *Delinquent Behaviour in an American City.* California: Wadsworth, 1970.

Gordon, M. *Penal Discipline.* London: Routledge, 1922.

Hall, R. *Ask Any Woman: a London Inquiry into Rape and Sexual Assault.* Bristol: Falling Wall Press Ltd., 1985.

Heidensohn, F. *Women and Crime.* London: MacMillan, 1985.

H.M. Chief Inspector of Prisons. Annual Reports, 1983-1987.

H.M. Chief Inspector of Prisons. *Report on H.M. Prison Holloway,* 1984.

H.M. Prison Service. *Holloway Project Committee Report,* July 1985.

Home Office. *Criminal Statistics England and Wales,* 1985, 86, 87.

Home Office. *Further Studies of Female Offenders.* Home Office Research Study No. 33, 1976.

Home Office. *Managing the Long-Term Prison System.* Report of the Control Review Committee, 1984.

Home Office. *Prison Statistics England and Wales,* 1986, 87.

Home Office. *Reports of the Prison Department,* 1980, 1982.

Home Office. *Report of the Work of the Prison Service,* 1986/87, 1987/88.

Home Office. *The Treatment of Women and Girls in Custody.* London: H.M.S.O., 1970.

House of Commons. Education, Arts and Home Office Sub-Committee. *Women in the Penal System.* London: H.M.S.O., 1979.

House of Commons Social Services Committee. *The Prison Medical Service.* Report 3, 1986.

King, M. *Bail or Custody.* Cobden Trust, 1971.

Leonard, E. *Women, Crime and Society.* London: Longman, 1982.

Mandaraka-Sheppard, A. *The Dynamics of Aggression in Women's Prisons in England.* London: Gower, 1986.

McConville, S. *The Use of Imprisonment.* London: Routledge Kegan Paul, 1975;

Matthews, J. *Women in the Penal System.* NACRO, 1981.

Matthews, J. *Forgotten Victims: How Prison Affects the Family.* NACRO, 1983.

Mawby, R. 'Sexual Discrimination and the Law' in *Probation Journal*, Vol. 24, 1977.

Mawby, R. *Women, Crime and Law Enforcement*. Unpublished paper, November, 1977.

Mental Health Act 1983.

Mental Health Amendment Act 1983.

Morgan, R. & R. King. *A Taste of Prison*. London: Routledge & Kegan Paul, 1976.

Morgan, R. & R. King. *The Future of the Prison System*. London: Gower, 1980.

Morris, A. & C. Wilkinson, eds. *Women and the Penal System*. Cropwood Conference Series No. 19, Cambridge 1988.

Morris, R. 'Attitudes towards Delinquency' in *British Journal of Criminology*, Vol. 5, 1965.

Morris, A. & L. Gelthorpe, eds. *Women and Crime*. Cambridge Institute of Criminology, 1981.

NACRO. *Prisoners in Police Cells*. Briefing Paper, 1st August, 1988.

NACRO. *The Future of Holloway: A Summary of the Special Project Committee Report*. Briefing Paper, 1985.

Nooney, K., L. Eastwood & I. Ray. *A Census of Mothers in Penal Institutions on 15 March 1982*. DPS Series II, No. 132, 1984.

P. d'Orban. 'Social and Psychiatric Aspects of Crime' in *Medicine, Science and the Law*, July 1972.

Padel, U. & P. Stevenson. *Insiders: Women's Experience of Prison*. London: Virago, 1988.

Parker, H., M. Casburn & D. Turnbull. *Receiving Juvenile Justice*. Oxford: Blackwell, 1981.

Patullo, P. *Judging Women*. National Council for Civil Liberties, 1983.

Peckham, A. *A Woman in custody*. London: Fontana, 1985.

Plotnikoff, J. *Prison Rules: A Working Guide*. Prison Reform Trust, 1986 and revised edition 1988.

Posen, I. *Holloway Officer Stress Study*. Holloway Psychology Department, 1984.

Posen, I. *Reception Survey, Holloway*. Holloway Psychology Department, 1987.

Prison Officer's Association. *'Prisoners' Rights - Real or Imagined ?'* 1986.

Prison Reform Trust. *Prison Medicine: Ideas on Health Care in Penal Establishments.* 1985.

Prison Reform Trust. *Remanding Juveniles.* Remand Project Paper No. 9, 1986.

Prison Reform Trust. *The Bail Lottery.* Remand Project Paper No. 8, 1986.

The Prison Rules, revised 1964.

Private Sector Involvement in the Remand System. Green Paper, Cm. 434, July 1988.

The Prosecution of Offences Act 1983

Punishment, Custody and the Community. Green Paper, Cm. 424, July 1988.

Radical Alternatives to Prison. *The Use of Drugs in Prison.* 1982.

Report of the Home Office & DHSS Interdepartmental Working Group on Mentally Disturbed Offenders in the Prison System in England and Wales, May 1987.

The Baroness Seear & Elaine Player. *Women in the Penal System,* Howard League for Penal Reform, 1986.

Self-Mutilation at Holloway. DPS Report Series II, 1974.

Shine, J. *A Description of Drug Offenders in Holloway.* Holloway Psychology Department, 1984.

Sloan, C. *A Study of Mothers and Infants in Holloway Prison.* DPS Report Series II, 1972.

Smart, C. *Women, Crime and Criminology.* London: Routledge & Kegan Paul, 1976.

Smith, R. 'Women in Prison' in *British Medical Journal,*Vol. 288, February 1984.

Steffensmeier, D. & R. Steffensmeier. 'Who reports shoplifters?' in *International Journal of Crime & Penology,* Vol. 5, 1977.

Stewart, C. *Fires in Holloway: A Survey of All Fires Occurring from February 1977 to November 1980.* DPS Report Series II, No. 120, 1983.

Stewart, C. *Disturbed women in Holloway.* Evidence for submission to the Committee on Mentally Abnormal Offenders, 1973.

Stewart, C. & J. Shine. *Disturbed Women in Holloway*. Holloway Psychology Department, 1985.

Vera Institute of Justice. 'The Manhattan Bail Project' in *Programs in Criminal Justice Reform*. Vera Institute of Justice Ten Year Report 1961-1971. New York, 1972.

Ward, D. & G. Kassebaum, *Women's Prisons*. London: Weidenfeld, 1965.

Warren, M. ed. *Comparing Male and Female Offenders*. London: Sage, 1981.

Lord Windlesham. 'Punishment and Prevention: The Inappropriate Prisoner' in *Criminal Law Review*, March 1988.

Winfield, M. *Lacking Conviction: The Remand System in England and Wales*. Prison Reform Trust, 1984.

Cases

Leech v. Dep. Gov. Parkhurst [1988] 2 WLR 290.

Raymond v. Honey [1982] 1 All E.R. 756.

R. V. Nottingham Justices, ex parte Davies [1980] 2 All E.R. 775.

Other Civil Liberties Trust titles

General
The Price of Justice, Howard Levenson, £2.95
Drifting Into a Law & Order Society, Stuart Hall, 95p
Right of Silence, James Wood & Adam Crawford
 (due for publication in February 1989), £2.95
The Accountability of the Security Services, Richard Norton-Taylor
 (due for publication April 1989), £2.95
Black Magistrates, Michael King & Colin May, £4.95

Policing & Criminal Procedure
Troops in Strikes, Steve Peak, £4.95
Police Authorities During the Miners' Strike, Sarah Spencer, £4.95
Controlling the Constable, Tony Jefferson & Roger Grimshaw, £7.95
Policing the Miners' Strike, (ed. Bob Fine & Robert Millar), £4.95
Incitement for Disaffection, (A Cobden Trust Study), £1.20

Northern Ireland
Supergrasses, Tony Gifford QC, £1.50
Abolishing the Diplock Court, S C Greer & A White, £3.95

Women's Rights
Judging Inequality, Alice Leonard, £9.95

Race, Nationality and Immigration
Immigration, Law and Practice, Lawrence Grant and Ian Martin,
£18.00
Immigration, Law and Practice (First Supplement), Lawrence Grant
and Ian Martin, £10.25
Towards a Just Immigration Policy, Michael King and Colin May,
£4.95